#METOO, NOW, WOMEN'S LIB, JUST SAY NO

Why they'll never work

Carolyn Franklin M. A.

Contents

It was a writing class for fledgling female writers. Sixteen of us hopeful authors critiqued each others' submissions.

There were poems, autobiographies, science fiction and romance for us to think about and consider our ideas and construction. The readings were interesting, but the poetry was pretty lame. Two women were trying to be thought-provoking by an awkward arrangement of words. Writing poetry requires an unfettered spirit and there's not many of those around.

The fiction writers dwell on the fates of "Hermione and Algernon" - will Algernon propose to his true love, Hermione Snidge? Or, will he do his duty as Lord of Plithing on Figbarre and betrothed to Genella d' Swithingham?

The ladies in the group can hardly contain their excitement at Algernon's dilemma.

My genre is diatribe, I am out to reform the world; I want to wake people up into a frenzy of social change. But, this category is not for the faint-hearted - perhaps for the fool-hearted, people who shovel sand against the tide, people who are deluded into thinking there is hope for improvement - the future holds peace and understanding, acceptance for all.

Dream on…

That day the draft of my reading was about an evening with Darryl, a long-time friend who was a good man, loyal, helpful, dependable and trustworthy. All good qualities. I liked him and appreciated him for those qualities. He was very much enamored of me and I am basically soft-hearted, so I had dinner with him maybe once a month. I did my best to make the evening pleasant for his sake.

I said, I "liked" him - I didn't "enjoy" him.

He was boring, *BORING*, **BORING**! There was only one topic Darryl had mastered, and that was, Darryl - all about Darryl. He had no interest in politics, science, social change, etc. He had "no opinions on nuthin'." The bottom line was there was no future as "two" of us because Darryl was not educated - I had nothing to relate to.

He did say he liked music. Since I'm a trained musician in the classics, I was excited that we had something in common. Happily, I asked, "What kind of music?" He looked at me blankly, "…kind?…of music…?" He didn't know there were "kinds" of music. That topic died a swift, painless death.

As soon as I told the ladies in the class there was no future for "us" because he was uneducated, the 15 women writers in concert put up a howl, "You can't reject him because he's not 'educated'! Education isn't just college! There's more to a person than education! You can't…, you can't…" They were mortally wounded that I suggested the thought of a man who, just because he lacked personality, education, he was therefore downgraded.

What they have not internalized is, I can say pretty much anything I want as long as it's not slanderous. I have every legal and moral right to my opinion and feelings. No one can tell me, "You can't say that!"

The result of my draft of the story was expected; it happens all the time. As soon as women perceive a man is being maligned, criticized or ridiculed, the women, in unison, set up a howl of anguish; they vehemently opposed my topic, as a Greek chorus the Furies rose up - I was "unfair," to Darryl. "You can't…!" "That's not…!" "But he…!" "How can you say…!" ad nauseam.

It was a typical female knee jerk reaction to criticism against a man. Almost always, whenever I state negative observations as to the behavior of some man - no matter how accurate - the women present will rise up in arms to defend him, explaining minutely how I am in error: "He has his side, too, you know." "Well, you can't say that!" "You can't judge someone on that basis!" "Well, they're *not all* like that!"

Well, actually, I can. I can "judge" someone on any basis I want to. The assessment may be in gross error, but nevertheless I have every right to criticize or judge someone on any criteria I want - as long as it's true or an opinion.

If my time, energy and creative ideas are not understood, not welcomed or criticized, I have very right to say I am annoyed, disappointed, bored and reject the whole caboodle.

But for me, the really sad part of this standard, tedious, female reaction was the fact that no one had asked my definition of "education." As one, the group assumed I meant college education. To me, that shows *their* level of education and *their* ability to reason - almost non extant.

Nor did it occur to them that I had every right to reject Darryl on whatever grounds I chose. Their perspective was that I should think about "him," be concerned about "him," - why?

College is one kind of education. "Life" - the ability to observe events, analyze them, critique them - judge them somewhat reasonably, and perhaps understand them is, for me, a more an in-depth, use-full education. It takes an innate ability to discern, analyze and comprehend the flaws and strengths of social interaction, and perhaps suggest ideas for behavioral traditions of disparate societies to a path of concord.

Also, my definition includes the ability to reason, "cause and effect" - at least make an attempt to reason; one can see the birth of an emerging problem and a probable solution to that problem. That - to me, is the ultimate "education."

We could include "common sense" in that definition - trial and error. My definition of "education" is broad and reasonable. It works for me.

If someone bores me, why should I lie about it? The women wanted me, for Darryl's sake, to "be sweet," agreeable, attentive, submissive - in other words be like them, sacrifice myself so Darryl can be happy.

Their correct response should be, "That's nice of you to care enough for Darryl to spend an evening with him. I'm sure he appreciates your company and attention." And, that's true. *He* was happy. Fine. That was my only goal, to make a pleasant evening for the two of us.

All this definition analysis is the basis of why, so far, women's groups focusing on "equality," or respect, will not work.

At the conclusion of this "diatribe" I will give you five reasons why women's lib will not work.

In my experience, the overwhelming majority of women support the behavior, goals, needs and opinions of men. Women, in general, tend to give men a great deal of room for error, but we particularly support a man's expectation of women - we do what the man wants us to do - support his opinion. We're trained to satisfy the male ego.

I have observed when a man speaks adversely about a woman, the other women expect *her* to change. Rarely have I heard criticism that the man may be wrong. In the very small anecdote about Darryl, the women stated that my needs were wrong - I should change - not him. Opinions and needs of women are often disregarded, censored or ridiculed as selfish, short-sighted… by women!

This warped, unbalanced negation of women is basic to the structure of the current and past society and is indicative of the future - "what was, will be." Tradition will outlast any obvious social inequities and need for common-sense reform.

Another glaring example of how women perceive women is by the program, "What Would You Do?" on TV Friday nights (in the Pacific Northwest), hosted by John Quinones.

A pre-planned scenario of social cruelty or unfairness, is put upon some innocent person to disgrace them or humiliate them. All the players are actors but the audience thinks it's an actual event. One group of people, all actors, torment another group of actors in some way that it appears to the unsuspecting TV audience that a glaring injustice is taking place. The premise of the program is to see if anyone is kind enough, secure enough or brave enough to step in and right the wrong.

In one scenario, two "frat" brothers were being "tormented," hazed, in a public park. They were tied down, hands behind their back and legs tied together. They had long tubes, one end inserted in their mouth and the other end had a funnel used to pour "alcohol" into the tube, forcing the boys to drink excessive amounts of "alcohol." The boys being "hazed" pretended to be afraid, protested and tried to fight off the forced consumption of alcohol and get free.

Some people walked by, glanced over at the action, saw the boys tied up being forced to swallow some liquid against their will, and continued on. These people were disinterested in someone's problem. But other passersby rushed over to help the boys get out of their predicament; they were concerned about the boys' being in distress and the seeming unfairness of the hazing. The boys were set free and comforted by both men and women.

The next set of actors was two girls being hazed. They were seated on the park lawn in the same area as the boys, by a sidewalk where they could easily be seen by passersby.

The girls had on bikinis, their hands and legs were tied behind their back. A large piece of duck tape was stuck over their mouth so they couldn't speak. They could "squeal" and shake their head violently.

The girls in charge appeared to dump "ice water" on them and made fun of them. The trapped girls squealed in "pain" and tried to get free. Their discomfort was obvious.

No one helped them. Several women strolled by and looked over at the two girls in "distress," but no woman, no man, even asked if there was anything wrong. The women glanced at the squealing, wriggling girls, and kept walking.

No one was interested in their distress. ***NO ONE!***

Even the host, John Quinones was surprised that *no one* had any interest in helping the girls!

I was not surprised - disappointed, yes. This indifference is indicative of much of the covert attitude of woman to woman.

There have been studies on how women will support other women who are suffering from emotional pain. Women gather in groups to succor another woman in emotional distress. This is wonderful.

But, you'll notice this kind of support is done in private - support for women is rarely done in public - on TV, tabloids, pulpit.

Recently, in the news, on two separate occasions, college girls had too much to drink and they were hauled, unconscious, to a private room where they were, allegedly, raped by college jocks. As the two helpless girls were carried into the rooms by "friends" - mostly females (!), everyone was laughing, joking and in general looking forward to making the unconscious girls to be fools (and, in a sense, they were).

The two episodes, although in different times, different places, were identical in the strategies to humiliate the girls. They were half carried and dragged, unconscious into a bedroom, put on the bed and the door was closed.

In one case several "jocks" visited the room with the door closed and the unconscious girl on the bed. In the other case she was shut in a room with one jock, the star football hero.

In the aftermath of that night the "violated" girls were shamed by their classmates and took the boys to court charging them with rape.

Because the boys were star athletes just having fun and the girls were unconscious, the charge of "rape" was perceived as hard to prove.

In both cases neither boy went to prison, but the two girls were shunned, ridiculed and so shamed - by other girls - that they changed schools and were traumatized by public censure. One family sold their home and moved away.

Sad to say, in general, women do not support women. So, how can we expect social change? If, by implicitly condoning the behavior, or, actively supporting "rape," - if we "understand" the needs and actions of men, how can we make changes as to the way we women are regarded and treated? Will we always see ourselves as not worth the trouble to reach out to help - make substantial social change?

We have to assume the girls knew there might be some kind of sexual activity at the "party" - that seems to be an expectation these days. The general concept of "party" is loud music, excessive alcohol, drugs and sex. Passing out and getting "raped" is just more of the fun…

The above scenarios demonstrate the ultimate insult and abuse in a woman's life. This ultimate, daily, expected abuse demonstrates a

BLATANT LACK OF RESPECT for OUR SELVES

This is a loud and clear covert message as to who we understand ourselves to be.

WE HAVE MET THE ENEMY AND HE IS US

In the Sept. 24, 2018 issue of Time Magazine it mentions 47% of American women are feminists. That means that 43% are not necessarily interested in supporting women's rights - *their own rights.* 5% of those interviewed were anti feminists…

Of the 47% who consider themselves feminists, I suggest half of them are active in words only, not in deeds. They talk a good story, but when it comes to action, they suddenly back down, hide in the middle of the crowd. They will gladly accept the perks the activists struggle for, but they'll back down if asked to take a verbal or physical stand in public.

This current surge for women's recognition, support and respect, will fade away the same as all the other women's attempts at reform, an awakening, clear thinking, intelligent discourse and common sense.

For every woman who understands that "equality" does not mean "control," "oppression," "hatred" and "rejection," a great many other women think we are bitter man haters, lesbians, unfulfilled, frigid, deranged and socially warped.

When a woman complains about a man's behavior toward her - when he's annoying her in some way, a common response is, "You just don't understand him..." Meaning, women aren't "fair" to the men; we need to try to understand them... sacrifice ourselves...be nice...be sweet...

As Garfield, the cat, states, "We have met the enemy and he is us." (Walt Kelly, "Pogo.")

As I understand the #MeToo movement is exactly that - me, too. One girl is molested by her boss or some powerful male figure and another girl steps in and says, "I was molested, too."

They pursue justice in the courts and, hopefully, send a strong message of "hands off!" to society.

But, for every girl who has the courage to challenge a man in court, there are hundreds who are concerned about retaliation, censure, loss of income, the specter of the "what if's..." and worse yet, fear of social rejection, disapproval and loneliness.

Our opposition is "us;" women are a house divided. Some women are pushing for change; other women want to status quo, tradition. Perhaps the main reason we avoid change is fear of: loss of status, loss of perceived security - general sense of confusion.

If, as a woman, you believe you're not getting the respect you deserve, let's find out what *you* may be doing "wrong." It's possible you are your own problem. As we go through this book let's count the ways, we women could improve.

For one thing, I have noticed we try too hard. We want to impress others with what we can do, how well we do it and how easy it is to succeed. We want people to understand we have it all and can do it all.

If this is true, why do we work so hard at telling everyone? Why don't we just *do* it?

Moving on.

SUFFRAGETTES 1870, 1920

Berkeley, 1970's. It was on the TV, one of those programs where a news-caster was interviewing Berkeley University college students to see what knowledge of American history they may have.

The interviewer approached a girl student in nondescript Berkeley laissez-faire attire - very casual, huge eye glasses, hair straggling over her face, blank expression and she was carrying books.

Thrusting the microphone in her face, he asked. "Excuse me Miss. I'd like your opinion on Women Suffrage. The government is going to make suffrage for women compulsory. What is your opinion on that?"

She was outraged! "They can't do that to us!" She clamped her mouth shut and shook her head violently, side to side.

I wasn't surprised. The newsman thanked her and moved on. As a college Instructor, I have found most of my students come to class tabula rasa; in so many cases when I have a concept to teach them, I have to give a lengthy "back story" and then segue into the actual course subject.

It's tedious.

In 1870, in England, women were granted the right to vote - suffrage. The date is approximate as there were many separate women's groups pushing for enfranchisement. This was a milestone in the rights of women.

In America, at the same time, the right to vote was granted to black men, but no women. It was at this time Sojourner Truth spoke before Congress explaining the logic of franchise for women.

She pointed out the obvious: Women worked as hard as the men, they ate food when they could get it and held their own in all phases of life - plus bear children.

Sojourner said that men are in a "tight place;" they're "between a hawk and a buzzard." She was a born orator and spoke English with a Dutch accent, very precise.

You may want to read her speech and I suggest the version by Marius Robinson 1851 in the Anti-Slavery Bugle. At this point in time, it's been 167 years since her speech and we still have the same line of patter; we did get the vote, but as far as recognition, respect goes, or pay equal to our ability, we have made embarrassingly little progress.

In America women's rights were very slow in moving ahead. Tireless, dedicated women leaders, Susan B. Anthony, Victoria Woodhull and Elizabeth Cady Stanton were three of hundreds of women who pushed constantly to impose rights for women on Congress, with no success.

In the push for rights, women were jailed and went on a hunger strike. They were tied down and force-fed through tubes. Many died from abuse in prison, but the cause slowly gained momentum.

Women of means, money, comfort, security, status, have almost no interest in other people who struggle to get through life. In general, women volunteer for charities - serve free lunches for the hungry, organize charitable fancy dress balls for the homeless, run the 25 mile marathon - in cute running shoes and pink top emblazoned in some logo that says they really do care - to help pay for scholarship college fees…

Yes, all good deeds, good causes, but these women are financially secure and comfortable in marriage and/or society. They keep a safe distance from the "others," the good deeds that they do, the charity they enlist, are a "hands-off" approach. Time and money are their contributions to help the "downtrodden."

They don't need an increase in pay to support their family or for the increase in rent. They already have respect and security for themselves.

Fighting for women's rights, actually being physically on site, submitting their name in public, would force them to associate with "losers," or women of questionable political leanings.

Women Democrats protest against Republican women; Pro Choice protests against Pro Life; pro female United States President against pro male tradition… the basic stance of women in politics is women against women.

In one club I belonged to, a socially traditional organization everyone, but me, was either a husband, wife or widow. They all agreed no one would vote for Dianne Feinstein or Nancy Pelosi. The women, in particular were vocally aggressive against them - no reason given, just against them. No intelligence required.

Surely, since we are all women, we must share the same anxieties and fears to some degree…? Why are we against each other instead of moving ahead, like a tsunami does? With united power we can accomplish much. Disjointed, pulling apart as we do solidifies the understanding that we are incapable of progress - timely progress.

The goal for all women should be the same thing - *respect.*

But we give the men much fodder for humor as they watch our "female hysterical" bickering. We do their job for them - we keep ourselves divided, provide the men with entertainment and grounds for not supporting us, not respecting us.

But, as in habit, tradition, ignorance, those women who stand against women

on controversial issues do so because they have been trained to obey men, the false gods, fear of loss of security. These women don't understand that with unity we have security.

We can be mothers; we can be housewives, we can be CEO's - we can be whatever we choose to be and know we are respected. If we stand together as women, wives and mothers; we can have the men, husbands, fathers, understand that deserting the family, walking away from fatherhood and responsibility, will not be tolerated - by society as a whole.

That to disrespect one woman is to disrespect us all.

United we can bring peace and unity to this amazing world.

Women who are comfortable with their lifestyle, who have recognition in society, a "position," who are "settled," will probably not be molested, cheated or downgraded because of their sex. There's no reason for affluent women to change any part of their status or habits.

Therefore the women who want to be treated equally in commerce and public are obligated to stand out of the crowd to demand recognition and respect.

Thea Iberall "We Did It For You"

In today's world of protests, demonstrations, live videos, where information is instant and any infractions of rules are immediately exposed on the media, women have no understanding of the hell that our predecessors suffered for us to have our legal rights and full recognition as citizens.

Dr, Thea Iberall created a musical play that takes us on a tour through the history of women's struggle for recognition and rights in America. Individually, the major historical personalities tell their part in the intense struggle to obtain what was rightfully ours.

At that time women protestors were hauled off to jail, hands tied behind their back and tied to chairs. They had gone on a hunger strike until they were awarded the right to vote. Tied down, they were force fed. The jailers poured raw eggs and milk into the women's noses which resulted in some women drowning.

They sacrificed their life so we, the future generations, could take our place in America, have our voice in the government, have the rights of all citizens. Until then *all* men had rights, but not a single woman.

Today we are insulated by time and much indulgence. To date there are laws that that are enacted to protect women from being molested, laws that protect us from being cheated, harmed and by-passed for justice.

But we have to be vigilant so we don't drift away from the intense dedication of our fore-mothers, sisters and friends. We have legal rights but we still experience molesting and humiliation, and, we have not done enough to stop it.

Rape, molestation, abuse are common, but rather than openly address them society covers them up, talks in whispers about them because they are a shame upon us - we women "asked" for it. These events are so ugly, we choose to hide them and hope they'll go away.

They won't. Some diseases require aggressive treatment.

NOW National Organization of Women 1966

Originally this organization was designed to call attention to the inequities of salaries for men and women. NOW wanted equal pay for equal work. This "demand" seems like a no-brainer to me.

Of course there was opposition, most of it fueled by tradition; men support families, men are better workers, men are easier to get along with, women have their "monthly problem," are hysterical - all fatuous excuses, people desperately trying to find reasons to support male superiority.

There are none.

In one heated discussion with a woman, I was supporting equal pay for equal work. That woman gave reasons why men deserve higher pay; she said they have families to support and children to provide for.

I said that no one forces them to get married or have children - they do that of their own free will. Women have children, too, to support. Their husbands walked out of the marriage and the responsibilities of a family. The women have no "free" will - they are trapped in a difficult situation.

Milking a cow does not require human gender; neither does putting a bolt on a shaft. Almost any job can be handled by any variety of trained individuals. In fact, sitting here, wracking my brain, I can't think of a single occupation that is mono-gender oriented. I hope there's no one reading this who is dense enough to snort and say, "Huh! What about being a father!!! - a woman can't do that!"

Being a "father" is not an "occupation," a "profession" - it's a gift.

Salaries in general are not yet totally balanced, but NOW did make some significant inroads into pay increases for women.

NOW was specifically created for women's rights. But, it has dropped us in favor of focusing on "equal rights for race, class and other issues of oppression." (Ms 1996)

That includes everyone! Define "oppression"! The overwhelming population of any country is "oppressed" - ask them! Even poor Melanie Trump is oppressed, the "most" bullied - ask her!

And, ask any American, theoretically we have no "class" in America!

So, what happened to "W" - women? Our thrust should be the "W," not "other issues!" There are enough "issues" for many, many more separate organizations! When your own organization dumps you, it is indicative of the pervasive lack of respect women have.

Where was NOW for Monica? For Christine? For Anita???

(I can't hear you.......)

TITLE IX 1972

This is a civil rights law, Education Amendment, passed in 1972 to ensure gender equality in all aspects of federally funded education.

"(It is to) emphasize the sexuality or sexual identity of an individual in a manner, which prevents the individual's access to the educational benefits, or opportunities of UHM (University of Hawaii at Manoa)."

Some people think that sexual harassment isn't a big deal, but it is a big deal. It is illegal.

This amendment was to make sure everyone in education was treated fairly. When I was a student at San Francisco State University in the '60's there was no such protection for students. In two of my classes the professors stated, "I do not give A's to girls." That's final!

One professor I reported to Admission - he gave me a B when I had all A's in his class. The woman at Admissions snarled at me and said, "He can give you any grade he wants!"

Also I had written to Brandeis for admittance on the basis I qualified for a scholarship. Brandeis replied, by letter, "We do not accept non-Jews, and, in particular we do not accept females." End of story. I read the letter, laughed and threw it away.

That's the way it was.

Not anymore

JUST SAY NO 1990

Are you serious?

Just say, "No?"

The innocence of this idea is so useless, impossible, meaningless - it's hard to believe she may have been serious.

This slogan was devised by Nancy Reagan, wife of the President of the United States of America, First Lady, wealthy, protected, respected, removed from Reality.

When she says "No," everyone listens.

But when the everyday woman says, "NO!" it comes out, "XZ!" - unintelligible to many males who have been trained to hear what they want to hear, and "NO!" is not in their vocabulary.

Men in locker rooms evidently have a communication code that is shared and understood only by that population. These men have an understanding that women desire them sexually to the point of being obsessed.

The word is passed along that when a woman says, "No," it's translated as, "She doesn't mean it; she wants it - she knows she does!" - a very different message than women think they're sending! We think "NO!" says it all, when, to a man, it means we've *acknowledged him* - it's a one-way street - she is acknowledging his prowess. He's got her attention!

Just recently I read where one occupation that has the most serious physical dangers for women and one that is little regarded, is where the hotel maids and women janitors who clean office buildings, especially at night, have no protection.

They work alone at night, sometimes in two's, but even so, their low-paid jobs and solitary working conditions make them prime targets for physical harm. Very often these women are single mothers, wives whose husbands have left for greener pastures, and the jobs are critical to their survival and that of their family.

These women are trying to build an organization that will provide a living wage and physical protection. I wish them well.

#METOO 2018

Let's look closely at the current women's movement, the #Metoo movement. Will it, too, fade away?

Probably. *No, inevitably.*

If the preceding observations and comments seem out of balance in this era of women's rights, look again. I'm asking women to listen and observe interaction between males and females, and females and females, today, in general.

Observe how often a woman will defend a man when he's said or done something to offend a woman. In general a woman takes the man's side in a controversy. A man will either defend a man, or say nothing. It's extremely rare for a man to defend a woman. He would have to be very strong in himself, total self-confidence.

At this moment there's a lot of publicity and activity about sexual harassment from company heads to the female employees. The daily TV news reveals numerous cases from physical groping to mental control of women employees in small businesses up to corporations. Wherever there's men and women, there's likely a problem of sexual harassing.

This is "news," and when the "new" gets old, it will be dropped, set aside, for any other information that sells their advertisers products.

Dr. Christine Ford was under crossfire from men and women. More likely than not, she's being truthful - it would be extremely difficult to fake that intensity of pain. But the women there in government, with status, will never help her - their own profession, their own standing in the community is at stake. If they want to keep their job they have to cooperate with the traditional power base - the men.

One day this, alleged, heinous attack, such as Christine suffered, may happen to their daughter and then they've set a precedent of accepting attacks, traumatizing a young girl to the point of blocking much of the details out. The people who tolerate attacks on girls are setting themselves up for a fall.

There is a God, karma, retribution - you reap what you sow!

The movement of MeToo (sans #) was started 10 years ago by a black woman, Tarana Burke, to encourage black women to speak out about physical abuse by their husbands or boyfriends. She was focused on educating black women to understand that they can get aid and change their lives if they want to.

Ms Burke offered support and guidance for a better way of life to a specific population which happened to be black women. Apparently, other people in that population either couldn't organize the women for some reason, or didn't have the determination and ability to face that daunting task.

Unfortunately, somewhere along the line black women picked up the notion the women's movements were for white women only.

White women, on the other hand, assumed "women" meant *anyone* who was not a man. And, I hasten to add, men are very welcome if they want to join in! We're not exclusive, just embroiled in our own needs. White women assumed we're all in this together - women are women - ask Sojourner Truth.

Did we white women send out a message of propriety? Where did that come from? What message did we send of "freedom and equality" - respect - for us, only? Did we suggest that respect was only for an exclusive part of the population?

Everyone deserves respect (*everyone!*) until they demonstrate otherwise. Differences in physical aspects are meaningless; no one person is more valuable than another. However, it's very difficult to respect someone who treats you badly and that situation is all too evident in our society - at many levels.

Some people are hateful because of an inner fear, life-conditioning, misunderstanding…so many reasons. But the result can be disastrous for all society. It's a chain reaction; you hurt me, I hurt the next person, he or she hurts the next 3 people…

Fear is the most dangerous element in anyone's life.

We women will never move ahead in society, or respect ourselves, until we open our eyes and ears to any business-as-usual negative gender interaction. To stand by while one woman gets insulted is to stand by while we all get insulted.

It requires diligence on the part of women - if we're the ones who are the brunt of a situation then it's up to us to unite, be vigilant to correct it.

Women who consider women-activists as "them" are doing themselves a disservice. We're all in this together; we have to stand up for those who want overall acceptance by society.

The women who are married today, whose husbands are present in the home and bring income for a comfortable life style, perhaps assume this is the way it will always be. They did the right thing, so their lives will continue along a predictable path. These women may be living on borrowed time.

I know a woman, whose husband provided well for her and the children. This woman played tennis (in her BIG yard) most mornings and bridge most afternoons. She went out to lunch often with her friends. Then, suddenly, her husband was arrested for embezzlement of company funds and is spending considerable time unavailable. They were divorced. She got a job in high tech and is doing well. No more tennis, no more bridge.

Another woman, was married to a vibrant, outgoing guy in his 40's. BOOM! Heart attack. Died, left her nothing. She married a much older man to have his pension to live on with her three kids.

A man at my church, who is very successful by today's standards, said, "If you do the right thing, the right thing will happen!" I was amused!

Yes, Virginia, there is a Santa Claus.

These scenarios are all too real and too possible for a woman's future - you and I.

Ask yourself, where will you be one year from now? Could you make it on today's pay for women?

It's odd, we Americans, make every effort to recognize and honor people of color, Asians, Native Americans, immigrants - but when it comes to gender - those who see a need to progress for one of our own - we question the wisdom, the motivation of those Americans who seek change.

Respect should be the *major goal* for all Americans, everyone, in America.

Have you noticed how many movements there have been to instill a sense of right in society for women? And no movements for rights for men? Why do you suppose that is?

Will women ever get to the place where we can be ourselves, just respect ourselves and not worry about what "he" thinks, or what "she" thinks of "me?"

Yes, Dorothy, it's a place over the rainbow where blue birds fly.

LOW SELF ESTEEM

By the Law of Averages, somewhere in this world is a person sitting with a beer in his hand, sitting on a beach, looking out over the ocean waves, just being quiet and happy with himself. He doesn't want a new car, a blonde, or insider trading. That is good self-esteem.

The main reason why women have not supported women in the past in the innumerable slights and insults we receive, is because we don't think we deserve better - we deserve to be humiliated and down-graded. We have been trained from the cradle to see ourselves as second class - or less.

It's so pointless and tiresome.

Maslow's Hierarchy of Needs .... Self-esteem

Abraham Maslow came up with the theory of how each person needs to develop into a whole person - that is someone who is satisfied with himself. (Let's ignore any gender pronouns.)

Maslow theorizes there are five Needs; the first four are "deficiency" needs. The last, and most difficult to achieve is referred to as "Self-fulfillment." (Actualization)

1. The lowest and broadest Need entails *Physical* needs: food, water, sleep and breathe fresh air. Without these basic life-sustaining ingredients, no one will survive.

2. After we breathe and sleep, our Need is a place to cook breakfast - a place of *Safety* where we can sit down and eat in peace, sleep well and not worry about mortar fire, floods or vampire bats.

3. When we're safe at home our Need is for someone to *Love* us, to assure us that we have value, we're wanted, and maybe are unique. We should feel comfortable at home, knowing that we're secure from all harm, protected.

4. At this stage of development we Need *Esteem*, a feeling of self-worth, accomplishment, value, importance. This is where we become cheer leaders, star athletes, MVP, the lead in the musical, prom queen. We feel loved - for the moment.

5. This stage is no longer a Need, but where we should all end up psychologically, "self-actualization." That's where we "don't care." If someone says, "Oh, you have a wart on the end of your nose!" - you don't care. "Sue got a raise and you didn't!" - you don't care. "Your kid bummed out in the Little Leagues," you don't care - you love him anyway.

"Self-actualization" is sometimes termed "self-realization"; it's the ability to make yourself "real" or "actual" - very New Age terms. You have no need to be jealous, hateful, resentful, hurt… because,

This 5th stage is considered the most important, but it's not. The 3rd, Need, is most critical in self development and self acceptance. If we're not secure in the home, safe, loved, cherished, encouraged, we have nothing to grow on; nothing to stand on, nothing to support us.

We float in space trying to find a landing, somewhere we can rest; somewhere we are assured in knowing we're doing the right thing. I think this is the "kitchen" of our nightmares where we dream up excuses, "cook up" escapes and goals to become a person of value. Only in dreams can we be who we see ourselves as, and that's not "real."

How many people have recurring dreams of flying? Perhaps they're looking for a "landing," a place to rest, to be secure. Maybe they're not "escaping" from something, but "looking" for something, going to… - a home, acceptance…?

We're told to "love yourself" - ok…how? Traditionally girls have no value. So where do you start self-esteem on a no-value chart?

This is a concept that has been beaten, literally, senseless. Innumerable books have been written promising ways to "build up inner strength, character, achieve success, heal inner wounds, liberate the inner child" - I even read one book that said we should 'assert' ourselves.

The problem is the books don't say "how" to do these things clearly, "tangibly."

If you go back to the source of the problem of lack of self esteem, you'll find it in a big book under Numbers 14:18 that says the sins of the father shall be visited upon the child.

This is interpreted any number of ways, depending on what religious training you've had. To me it means if your grandparents screwed up your parents, your parents will, probably, screw you up in some way, too.

If boys were regarded as superior to girls in their generation, that concept will, probably, be blanketed on the following generations. It's an old-wives' tale that is pervasive in society. It's embarrassing that today we can fly to the moon with current technology, yet we still hold fast to the idiocy that one gender is better than another.

In one of my little jobs to get me through school I worked at a business where I had to take care of lockers with combination locks. A woman about 70ish came up to me, her lower lip quivering and tears in her eyes. "My husband, John, always worked the combination... I don't know how. I can't get in the box." More tears. I was disgusted! Here is a woman, in her 70's who can't work a combination! I said, "C'mon." and started toward the lockers. "Oh," she brightened up. "Are you going to do it for me?!" "No, you are." Stunned, she followed me. We stood in front of the lock; I said, "Go right 3 times. Now go 1 1/2 times left, now go right and open." She did and it did. She was elated.

How can a woman grow older and never have worked a combination? She was crippled by tradition - she was always told, you need a man for that! Women can't... fill in the blanks. I hear this so often; we train women to be mental cripples. Then, of course we have little self-esteem, if any.

HOW TO WORK ON SELF-ESTEEM..(my 2 cents)

First. stop explaining yourself!

You owe no one any explanations for your behavior, your choices, your hobbies, your tattoo's - only the IRS can pin you down and then you can always compromise. The IRS sometimes has more heart than you think!

When people judge you

When someone asks, "Why do you…?"What did you…?

When, how, who…?

How are you…?

What if you…?

Why don't you…?

Are you going to wear, do, see, read, eat…..that?

They're trying to pin you down, put you on the defensive, control you, manipulate you. Don't allow that. You have the power, and right, to put it back in their court.

Simply respond with another question: "Why?"

Sit back, relax and wait.

Stop excusing others: People do what they do because they want to!

When someone keeps you waiting, borrows money, breaks something of yours, lies about you, forgets to do something you need…

laughs at you…

Don't make excuses for them:

> Well, that's the way he is.
>
> Well, she's having a hard time.
>
> He would if he could.
>
> I'm sure he didn't mean it.
>
> He'll make it up to me.
>
> She meant to, but…
>
> But, he promised!
>
> Oh, well.. I should have…
>
> Maybe if I didn't…
>
> Maybe I misunderstood…
>
> All he needs is a chance! (I've often wondered, a chance to…what?")

These kinds of excuses pave the way for more of the same unacceptable behavior. You can either stop seeing these people or cut back on interaction.

Stop being defensive

To "be defensive" is to explain why you did, didn't, should have…do something.

Stop explaining your actions, beliefs, opinions to anyone.

If they don't agree, if they don't like something you do, they don't have to! And, you don't have to change!

> *I had dinner at someone's home and she loudly complained that I put salt on my food before I tasted it. I asked her how my salt preferences altered the course of her life. She was very annoyed at my insolence. And, sadly the other women at the dinner were also annoyed with me.*
>
> *I'm still trying to figure out why.*
>
> *Are there specific rules as to salt consumption?*

We don't need to "increase" self esteem; we only need to focus on our strengths to charge the esteem we have. We all have lots of "good stuff" going on that we need to honor - use it!

Help others

Get your mind off yourself. There are so many people who need your expertise, a kind word, a helping hand… Stop wallowing in "poor me." There are many people in many places that need you - and would trade places with you in a split second!

Count your blessings, count them one by one…

Most of all we need to focus on good character. You can't see good character; you can't measure it - you intuit it; you know that it's there. What else matters? Very few of us will be Bill Gates, Napoleon, the guy next door with the new car…nice house…

Who cares?

Believe me they have their problems too - if not more so. Are you looking for admiration? Esteem in your neighborhood? Be top jock? It ain't always as good as it looks - "be careful what you wish for - you might get it!"

Stop comparing yourself to others

When I was a child age 5, I had a cousin, age 8, who was very pretty, always was pretty until her last days. I was smart. When we were standing beside each other, which was often, someone would say to her, "My, you're so pretty!" And then they'd turn to me and say, "Your so smart!" (This was quite impressive when said with our Massachusetts' accent: Yaw so pretty, yaw so smaaht…)

So Dolores grew up thinking she was dumb- she wasn't! She was very intelligent, artistic and had a great sense of humor.

And I grew up thinking I was ugly. Well, I wasn't ugly, but sure not beautiful. But, I was smart and still have a few marbles intact.

Dolores and I spent much time in combat, each trying to outdo the other, each thinking up ways to be better than the other one. What a waste of time! She'll end up in heaven with all the beautiful angels and I'll end up in the crossword puzzle department.

Comparisons are invalid. People compare others on what is important to them, and, that's usually something they lack. They see in others what they don't see in themselves. The paradox is, we already have what we admire in others - we're just not using it as much as someone else is!

There are no two humans exactly alike. I have twins and they're very different.

Just be yourself and like yourself - you're one-of-a-kind! Stop comparing yourself with a friend, a neighbor, a rock star. Comparisons are lethal to our psyche and warp our vision of self. To compare ourself to anyone else is to look into one of the mirrors that distort our image - our head is 2 feet high and our feet are under our chin. We laugh and move on.

So, stop comparing yourself to a distorted mirror. Focus on being a great, kind, honest person. That'll win a lot of points!

There will always be someone better than you at something, and some one worse - why bother to get involved? Just let it be.

I had a close friend who was very talented and beautiful and popular. I was so jealous. In spite of my jealousy we spent a great deal of time together and had so much fun. She died in her 40's of cancer. I miss her so much and I'm sad when I think how I envied her. I should have just enjoyed our friendship.

It was a party at church, I was about 14 and sat next to a pretty girl the same age. I hated her - she was pretty! I ignored her. Then, something happened, I couldn't resist leaning over and saying something funny about it. She burst out laughing, relieved that someone spoke to her. It was at that moment I realized pretty girls have feelings, too. I like them now.

People will ridicule you, make fun of you, put you down, and, when they do, don't smile. Don't say anything; don't encourage it. Women do this, men too, but women mostly. Don't feed into it. If possible leave, and don't see those people again. It's better to have no friends than ones who hurt you.

Your "Schadenfreude" (<u>shah</u> den <u>froy</u> duh) is almost always a female

Some of us have a "schadenfreude" a harm-joy friend. This is a friend who is secretly jealous of you but pretends to like you. Don't be fooled. She will try to break you. She lifts you up with one hand and knocks you down with the other.

You just gave your dissertation for a scholarship. Your schadenfreude asks you, sounding very concerned, "Did you pass your exam?"

You smile and say, "Yes."

Schadenfreude says "Oh…" seemingly surprised. You get worried, what's wrong? Did you pass it wrong? Did you take the wrong test? What's wrong?

Schadenfreude says, "Oh, no…, that's great…," sounding dubious…

The "power" moment The moment you are free from opinions and judgement of *yourself* - and others.

Gloria Steinem in her book "Self Esteem," talks about a moment when you suddenly understand your own value and you stop comparing yourself to others. Your self worth takes a huge boost at that moment - it's like the "aha!" moment in research.

> *I was sitting at my desk thinking of all the people of the past who had affected me deeply in one way or another. In high school, the girl I thought was my best friend unceremoniously dumped me and walked off with another "friend." I fled to the girls' room and sobbed a river of tears.*

I thought of the people who liked me and wondered why - why would anyone like me? I have nothing to like. My mother hated me, my father left us and forgot us. I had to hide from my stepfather - he was a molester. I used to confide in my dog, my only friend.

One day, I sat deep in thought about what to do, how I should proceed in life with no friends; I was so alone.

Then, suddenly, I got the oddest feeling; nothing mattered! I felt a weight slip off my back; and then, nothing mattered!

I didn't care if I were liked or not! I really didn't! For some inexplicable reason, I was free! Free from others' opinions of me - and my own!

People weren't going to change for me - why should I change for them?! What could anyone do to me? Nothing! People could only hurt me if I let them! I had power over my mind! I had power over my thoughts, feelings, decisions -

I smiled! I was free!

That's self esteem, when you let go of the opinions and warped perception of

others. Some people will like you, some won't. They have a right to their feelings and you have the right to reject them.

Read Gloria Steinem's book, "Revolution From Within," a book of self esteem.

Very well done.

LONELINESS

Let's address "loneliness" at this point. In Life, there are no guarantees. Each day carries lumps and blessings. At times, when we've planned for a secure, socially approved life, marriage, children, grandchildren, our plans melt in a bonfire of shock and disbelief - what happened?

Life changes. Situations morph into a disfigured vision in the future.

Most women, girls, are trained for, and are expected to marry and have children. We look forward to the day we put on that gorgeous gown, the center of happy attention, and promise to love and care for someone until we die.

And we really mean it.

But… sometimes we don't die and the one we care for cares for someone else.

In Life, there's a real possibility you may end up alone. The divorce rate - depending on what stats you use, is 69% in America.

And, in this possible event, we want to be sure we can survive both socially and economically. As it stands today, the economic aspect is still not secure as far as the future looks - specifically for women. We are still underpaid, under promoted, betrayed and downgraded, often by our own sex.

A man I knew was a widower and he moved to complex of widows and widowers. He was relatively unscathed by time and so became a hot topic of interest to the throng of old, lonely ladies. Two widows went into combat for the charms of this elderly gentleman. One of them won him and, as she was making elaborate wedding plans, he died. There went her future - blown away!

Out of fear of loneliness we women often sell ourselves short, "settle for what we can get" so we'll have companionship in our senior years. I have seen women scrambling for security, reach out for "a" man - any man, so they can be assured of care and company at some indefinite future time. However, the future is always a lo-o-ong way off.

FEAR OF CHANGE

Fear of change is irrational - a state of mind - it is *not reality*. We women should want change, embrace it, want to be upgraded for recognition of our individual and collective value. We are not hoping to oust males; we don't want to replace men, or *be* men. We're glad men are men; we like men! We want everyone - men *and* women, to be treated equally under the law - with respect.

Well, not just "under the law;" we want everyone to be treated with respect because it's the right thing to do.

Is that wrong? Do we expect too much? Actually, it makes perfectly good sense. We need each other.

Women who are against recognizing women for intelligence and accomplishments, seem to understand Women's Lib is a reach for "power," control, to demolish men.

Those women define "respect" as cover for "power;" but it has nothing to do with "power." Some of the most "powerful" women in history were very feminine and appeared submissive. They put on a great act! But that's just one of our gifts!

The movement of MeToo (sans #) was started 10 years ago by Tarana Burke, creator of "Ebony Magazine. The magazine was designed to encourage young black women to reach out to each other and support each other. Ms. Burke, as a black woman wanted black women in general to speak out about any physical abuse by their husbands or boyfriends. She wanted to educate black women to understand they had the means and with determination they could get help to improve their lives. There were resources for help and education if they wanted to take care of themselves.

> *My supervisor at one time was an older black woman. She would listen to you, think about what was said, respond intelligently and, in general a woman I admired and appreciated working for.*

> *One of my duties was to answer the phone; a man called in and asked to speak to her. As is common, I asked him, "Who is calling please?" He responded, "None of your damn business!"*

> *Shocked I gave her the phone and said, "This man is incredibly rude!" It was her husband. She just shrugged her shoulders.*

> *His comment was entirely unnecessary. What must her home life be like?*

> *She was treated very rudely by the other male supervisors; really hurt my feelings.*

Ms Tarana Burke wanted to show black women there's a better way to live life than the one they may be dealing with. These women seem to be afraid to reach out for help and ask for guidance and support to change and improve their life conditions.

Other black women were reluctant to organize them because old habits and beliefs in the community were very hard to change. Apparently it was going to take an overwhelming amount of energy to educate and guide that group.

Unfortunately, black women seemed to think that developing inner strength and changing their environment was a goal only for white women.

White women, on the other hand, thought the movement was for all women - *anyone* who was not a man. White women didn't take specific notice of the low numbers of black women joining as they assumed everyone understood their purpose.

And, I hasten to add, men are very welcome if they want to join in! We're not exclusive, just embroiled in our own needs. White women assume we're all in this together.

Did we white women send out a message of propriety? Where did that come from? What message did we send a limited amount of "freedom and equality" - respect? That respect was only for an exclusive part of the population?

Everyone deserves respect (*everyone!*) until they demonstrate otherwise. Differences in physical aspects are meaningless; no one person is more valuable than another. It's very difficult to respect someone who treats you badly and that situation is all too evident in our society - at many levels.

Some people are hateful because of an inner fear, life-conditioning, misunderstanding…so many reasons. But the result can be disastrous for all society. It's a chain reaction; you hurt me, I hurt the next person, he or she hurts the next 3 people…

Fear is the most dangerous element in anyone's life.

On the Sundays at the Milpitas (California) jail for women, when I gave the talks, the congregation was about 1/2 Black and 1/2 White women. All of them either petty thieves or incarcerated for prostitution or selling drugs - to please their boyfriends. None of them were the stereotypical "criminals" - dangerous law breakers.

Most of them were mothers with their children farmed out here and there. One woman had 10 children in various homes. She was concerned about them and missed them. She was there for selling drugs for her pimp.

I found her attitude interesting. She was subdued; she seemed to understand her life was a dead-end; being incarcerated was just a momentary inconvenience. She understood her life was one of hopelessness, uselessness. When she's released, it's back to the same old grind.

I felt so sad for her.

These women didn't know about their right to self- respect. They were raised with the understanding their purpose - and survival, was based on serving and pleasing a man. They were limited in their outlook; there was no concept of a future of self-development - no self esteem.

> *At a Christian retreat for women, Cursillo (little courses, lessons in Christ), I was one of the counselors. The purpose of the retreat was to demonstrate "agape," unconditional love as Christ taught. After some time passed, a woman asked me, "When is someone going to 'love' me?" I said, "Oh, you've got it all wrong; no one's going to love <u>you</u>, you have to love <u>them</u>." She frowned.*

She could try loving herself - stop looking outside for approval.

As an aside, the *correct* pronunciation for "agape" is: "ah **GAH** pay" - exactly like that (unconditional love).

MONICA LEWINSKI, ANITA HILL

These two women made it big in the news. They were both the butt of jokes, betrayed by tradition. Where were the organizations of outraged women, fighting mad, ready to take up arms in defense of these two, ridiculed, injured women?

Where were the moralistic, stiff-necked women who right a wrong?

I'm still wondering and it's been years since the incidents.

Monica Lewinski

Era of 1998: Monica was betrayed by a close "friend"; how often do women betray their women friends? - let me count the ways! Monica confided her dilemma concerning the President of the United States, Bill Clinton, to a trusted friend. Apparently Bill was being pleasured by Monica and he was not reciprocating. She told her close friend, Linda Tripp about the situation and Linda told the world!

What a rotten "friend" Linda was! And, how many times does this happen? I often wonder what Linda expected to get out of betraying her friend? How did that improve her life?

So Monica had sex with a married man - he was married - she wasn't! Yet he wasn't censored - she was.

Like countless young girls, Monica trusted a man - the President! Who wouldn't trust "our" President! He probably said he loved her, he'd leave his wife, but she won't give him a divorce…Monica (insert girl's name of the moment) means everything to him…these are worn-out lines from every B movie and every door-to-door salesman from the beginning of time.

There is some speculation that America actually pursued a war in Chechnya at the time of the Clinton/Lewinski transgression. Do you think this war was coincidental to the affair? There are many people who seem to agree that this war was created to distract attention off Bill and Monica. The scandal of their liaison seems short-lived. And the war was not all that costly in money and lives.

Only a few people were slaughtered. At least it took our mind off that naughty boy!

My question is, why are girls allowed to wander through life without being forewarned about trickery and deceit? Advertising is rift with promises, lies of youth and beauty, eternal love from SWMD (seeks happiness and camping) in the tabloids. Would the tabloids lie?

As with Clinton, we smirked and nudged elbows at his cleverness at duping girls to trust him and let him "have his way." Clever fellow, eh?! But Monica! Who cares about her? She served her purpose. Let's forgive Bill and forget. Move on.

Next time it will be you.

Anita Hill

In 1991 Dr. Hill was Attorney-advisor to Clarence Thomas when he was nominated as Justice to the Supreme Court by George Bush. All went well until Dr. Hill was called to testify against Clarence for sexual harassment.

At the Clarence Thomas hearing, she was subjected to embarrassing, humiliating and ludicrous questions put to her by (now Vice President) then, Senator Joe Biden. Apparently Bush assumed Clarence was a shoe-in and wanted Dr. Hill quashed.

Joe clumsily bumbled through the humiliating charade of questions designed to make a joke of Dr. Hill's testimony. Ted Kennedy sat next to Joe and struggled to keep a straight face - it seems he was highly entertained - but, then, you know the reputation of the Kennedy boys!

Again, and again, where were the women's liberation movements? Where was the outcry of the shoddy, blatant, clumsy treatment of that highly educated, dignified lady? Who was in her corner with the microphone and visible support?

It's understandable that we don't support Monica, she was a kid, we can throw her to the wolves. Who cares - she's not my daughter!

But Anita was a prize in our society of educated, class-act achievers. If we don't support women like her, we women are committing genocide.

Aly Raisman

Aly is a three-time Olympic Gold medal winner, two golds in 2012, and the third in 2016. Besides being a star athlete, Aly was an outspoken accuser of Dr. Larry Nassar, official Olympic Team doctor. Dr. Nassar had molested160 girls over a period of years.

His abuse had been reported to the Committee, but the complaints were ignored. In 2018 Raisman made a formal complaint against Dr. Nassar and mostly because (of her gold medals - reputation) her testimony and courage in exposing him, he is currently serving 175 years in prison.

She is to be praised for her part in uplifting and empowering women in sports and in general from predators on children.

Then, in February of 2018, Aly posed nude for the Sports Illustrated Swimsuit Issue. She said that, posing nude for a magazine, whose customer sales are 3.2 million copies specifically designed for the titillation of men, "empowered" her.

She is quoted as saying, "Women do not have to be modest to be respected."

That's true - ask any porn star; they're not modest and we all know how well they're respected - the world "slut" comes to mind… available…?…easy?

Her thoughtful example of behavior will surely deter millions of girls from being leered at, groped and raped.

Thank you, Aly, for setting "respect" back to the Dark Ages.

ALEX

Alex, my student sat across from me, dejected. He didn't see the humor in what he said. A man wouldn't - this was no laughing matter. As far as I knew him, Alex had all the qualities of a good husband. He was anxious for marriage and a family.

He had a good job, was interested in what someone was saying, listened and responded appropriately; he was nice looking, good manners, a well-educated engineer with his own start-up in Silicon Valley.

What's not to like.

Alex is from India, spoke American English well, shy, reserved, courteous, but not used to "putting himself out there." He didn't know how to "wow the crowd" - he was more or less in the background, the "chorus," not a "star."

He'd been to "mixers," dating sites, blind dates, computer dating - but, no luck. He couldn't get a third, and sometimes, a second date. He did all the right things, took his date out to dinner at high-end restaurants, offered to take her to shows - whatever she wanted, Alex was happy to please his date.

Women didn't seem to respond to him. He put himself "out there" so he'd be noticed and hoped women to see he was available. But, at this time, "Love," the little arrow that strikes the heart was not sent to Alex; it was fast in the quiver.

Since he was not affiliated with a specific Christian denomination, I suggested he make the rounds of churches to meet a suitable woman who would understand his sincerity.

But, since *he* was a sincere person, he wouldn't go "wife shopping" at a church - he felt that wasn't honest. Maybe not, but…when you're lonely and a good person "don't hide your light under a basket" - "make a joyful noise."

Downcast, he stared blankly at the floor. With a deep sigh of resignation

Alex said, "I guess the girls all want rich, white men…"

This comment caused me to laugh; "Not really! Of course, if a rich, white man crossed my path and wanted to sweep me off my feet, I'd probably let him!"

But…I hope someday society will get to the point where we stop blaming white men for our own inadequacies. Usually, white men go to school, study, get degrees, start companies or get good jobs, work hard, and, instead of praising them for their initiative and dedication, too often we see their hard-earned success as selfish and a closed society.

And, usually, *it is a closed society.*

It seems from reading and hearing negative comments about the "success" of white men, how they achieved their status and security on the backs of others - they're unfair; that conclusion is largely based on jealousy.

Some people want the same success and status that white men have, but they don't want to work for it, spend hours strategizing, planning and studying for the same success white men have.

But…

Anyone can be successful; all they need to do for the same results is to do the same preparation. Even women can follow this example!

Then Alex asked what was the #MeToo movement all about. With so many "movements," women's organizations and seeming anger toward men, Alex is concerned he'll be hated or shut out from the society of women in general.

I explained #MeToo is a group of women who want respect - that's all, just the respect that any person deserves. They are not there to be used, handled, insulted, shamed or ridiculed. Women are angry in general because for far too long their abuse and humiliation has been arbitrary, encouraged, tolerated; we're often the butt of jokes and we're ignored by the media and the courts.

Again Alex sighed. "I guess I'm just caught in the crossfire."

On two occasions I had sued male defendants for money in small claims court. One man crashed into my car, the other refused to honor a warranty on a broken, new transmission.

*In both cases the defendants had **no evidence - none** I had receipts, contracts, witnesses, and dated reports.*

In both cases the male judges found for the defendants. I was stunned!

THE TROUBLE WITH SONS IS THEIR MOTHER

One of my close friends has 3 sons and one daughter. One day we were discussing her children and she said, "The trouble with sons is their mother."

I gave that comment a lot of thought. In my family of cousins, all the sons were chosen first for any treat and were spoken to in great reverence. We girls were well-treated, but not as good as the boys. I could tell something was haywire, but I couldn't figure out what. I never mentioned my confusion to them at the time - didn't seem like a good idea.

For example, two of my cousins, brother and sister, came home to lunch from school. The boy was about 6, the girl 8. The boy was fed in the house at the table, the girl was fed out on the porch steps.

When they both inherited money, the boy said, "My sister's mad at me over the inheritance - we're not speaking."

Surprised, I asked, "Why?"

"Because I got most of the money."

Surprised, I asked, 'Why?"

"Because I'm the guy."

She had mentioned this to me when she was in her 40's - she was still fuming; it hurt so bad. I couldn't understand fully at the time what she was saying - it was so wrong. I could go on with a litany of mistreatment, blatant inequities of how girls are treated in homes. But it's pointless. And, yes, in many cases boys are badly treated, too. What gain is there by mistreating children? What does that teach them?

Either way this breaks my heart.

MY FAVORITE SON

Across the world, since the advent of history, societies, cultures and tribes have revered the males. Males were held in esteem and elevated to superior beings in their culture whether they qualified or not.

There have been, and still are, small units of tribes where the woman is the boss:

The Mosuo of China, the Minangkaabau of Indonesia, the Bribri of Costa Rica and the Akan of Ghana.

Ever hear of them before? No? Apparently there are no wars or capitalism in those communities. Therefore nothing to write home about. They just get along…boring!

The Amazon women really existed. They were expert archers, warriors and killed their newborn sons - very much like China does with girls today. But, since they were a relatively small tribe, they were eventually overcome by male warriors and obliterated.

In general, women have accepted the male as the superior person in almost all societies. Freedom of expression and equality crusades in America are unusual; women of other cultures find us hard to understand.

Often a student of mine will become a personal friend. I was at lunch with Corey who was discussing her brother. "My

parents already told me they're leaving everything to him."
She said. There was a bitter edge to her voice. There was
just the two children, Corey and her brother. She rarely
mentioned her parents and had found a surrogate mother,
an elderly, Italian woman who lavished affection on her.
Corey and I spent time together as we could. I felt so sad for
her.

I have a long-time friend, Arlene, who has 4 sisters and one
"baby" brother. When the mother was elderly, the five
sisters took care of her for years alternating homes every six
months. The boy rarely came to see her. When she died, she
left everything to her son.

THE "MAMMONI"

"Mammoni" is an Italian word roughly translated as "Mommies'
boys."

There is a new breed of men - well, actually not "new" - just
more so - in Italy. The recognition of independence of Italian men
has long been accepted, but today this life-style is causing a
serious problem.

Since a man, preferably a husband, is the prize for women in
most cultures, women vie for attention; they vie for the
companionship and guidance of a man. The women cook meals,
accommodate themselves to the man's moods and needs, dress
beautifully, fix their hair - you know the routine - to "catch" a
man.

Therefore, Italian men have decided rather than get married, it's
more fun to play the "just try and catch me" game. Of course,
they're staying single - and winning at the game!

In Italy the birth rate has dropped considerably. Young men live at home where their mothers take care of them - Mommie does their laundry, cooks their meals, accommodates their every wish - why get married? They'd be fools to do so. They can have their pasta and eat it, too.

Italian mothers love their boys and they want grandchildren, but there's none in the horizon.

Meanwhile, Italian girls compete fiercely for a man - just like we do in America. If they can catch an Italian man that's a real achievement! A gold medal for them!

So unnecessary. Let men "catch" *you!*

All the girls have to do is play it cool and the boys will come running. Play hard to get and stand back. The rush to "get a girl" is inevitable. When you make yourself available, it's too easy; men like a challenge, whether in Naples or the Bronx.

I was on a large, tourist boat leisurely floating down the Nile. The evening was cool; several of us were sitting, chatting in Spanish, on the top deck under a canopy of glittering stars. A gentle breeze stirred the air around the center of attention, an incredibly beautiful girl from Spain.

The caste of characters were myself, 6 waiters and the stunning young lady; she was, maybe 20, 21 years old. The waiters mostly stared at her, captivated by her beauty, frozen in time and space.

She had on no makeup, no "base," no blending of shades of colors to enhance her eyes, no fake plastic lashes, no extensions, no eye shadow - nothing! It was all her youth and beauty - and modesty!

It seems that youth and beauty are the main attractions to establish self-respect. Well, it's good to have those attributes, but not all of us are blessed with devastating cheek bones and long lashes. And, for such a brief time are we young.

What the basic element of beauty and charm is - self respect, self-acceptance. We women have to do it for ourselves. No one is going to "give" us anything - we have to assume it, use it, remember it, live it.

Dignity and self-respect are the same thing.

By the way, as an aside, I have found out what men readily respond to is a compliment. Not on their clothes or looks - they're used to that, but on something they have casually done and took for granted.

If a man gives a report on some issue, mention to him how well organized it was, say how well he sounded making the points. When he parks the car - how well

he slipped into the space - like an "Indy" driver. When (and, if) he holds a door open for you, make it a point to - briefly - look into his eyes and say, "Thank you."

These little courtesies go a long way in establishing good rapport and respect for you both. Respect is not a one-way street.

MALE BONDING

Men like each other; they support each other - they bond. When a problem arises that concerns women - the "outsiders" - men close ranks, shut down communication. Have you ever noticed that when a woman is in distress, often she's alone in her problem? At that moment she has no dedicated allies, no one comes to her aid. She stands alone in the arena to survive, or not. Who cares?

Many men don't see a problem and, *don't care*. No one ridicules them. They don't ridicule each other - they don't censure each other - what's the big deal?

The classroom where I was teaching was directly over an alley. With the classroom windows open every word spoken in the alley was magnified and reverberated through the room.

*Her sobs were juicy and copious, "How **COULD** you do this to me!! How could you **DO** this to me? How could you do this to **ME**? (repeat ad infinitum)."*

I glanced out the window. She was wracked in sobs; he was sitting there looking up at the clouds, totally indifferent.

I thought, "Here she goes, full-speed ahead on the merry-go-round of futile relationships." No self-respect.

Perhaps the greatest gift men have, their greatest "skill," is not listening. Men instinctively shut down at the sound of a woman's voice, or a woman's needs. It's not that they don't care; it's just that they're not involved enough to care.

When a man molests, hurts, betrays a woman, it's not necessarily calculated - things happen. Therefore when a woman rejects a man's advances or sues him for some infraction of behavioral code, he may be genuinely caught off-guard.

And women invest their lives in wondering how they can please a man and keep him. What does that say about respect - for ourselves?

It was on the evening news. A masked robber ran into a hardware store. There was a woman customer and two male clerks, one in his 40's another in his 60's. The woman was standing between the robber and the cash register. The robber started beating on the woman. She was bent backward from the blows with her hands up covering her face. The two men clerks stood close together watching the woman get hit. The two of them were safe, in an area stocked with hammers and large, iron tools. The robber finally stopped the beating, grabbed money out of the cash register and ran out.

Men have an innate gift of removing themselves from any emotional involvement, be it guilt, fault, inadequacy and total introspection. In general they don't have the mechanism for regret or guilt .

When I taught at Foothill College in

*Los Altos, I entered a classroom with my students and there was a young man already there using our computers. I had the Midterm scheduled that day so I asked the odd student to please leave my classroom. He didn't even look up, but responded with "**F... YOU!!!**" It took me moment to recover! Again, I asked him to please leave my classroom and again received the curt, rude, disrespectful comment.*

He did leave but my students missed 20 minutes of their time for the Midterm. I took him before the school Governing Board for discipline. The Board was comprised of two students and one professor, all males. I was there with my witness, a secretary, female, who heard the whole event,

I explained my position to the Board; my witness described her position and the student explained his side.

I wanted him expelled.

But, true to tradition, the men formed an alliance. The three boys looked at each other, silently, for a moment, then one of them told the offender, "We have decided you cannot attend any parties until after this quarter is over. Do you agree?"

He agreed, and then they all walked out in a good mood.

I was stunned! That was a slap in the face! Male bonding.

So I'm asking the women in these altruistic movements, "Do you really, seriously think, for one second, that men will ever allow us to stand beside them? Do you really think men will respect us and let us have a place beside them, let us share decision-making?

Open your eyes and your mind. See what's obvious; stop excusing bad behavior and expect it to change - it won't. It's their make-up to set-up, aim and fire! They hold the gun - tradition; they win.

Women need to take the gun away and put in the closet, up high, behind the Christmas wrappings - no better yet, put it away in the closet with all the house-cleaning supplies; that's the last place a man would look for anything.

As far as "giving us" our rights, no one will ever *give us* anything - we have to *take them.* We don't need to "grab them," wrestle our rights out of someone's grip; we unite, agree on the direction, gently release any problems and continue on our path.

We teach children to share, adults should do the same. By that I mean legally and without looking back. Men all too often are sore losers. But, they'll get over it. Actually, I'm happy to share anything as long as I get half - that's enough for me.

This women's movement does not need to be antagonistic or heavy handed - just steady and determined. We all need to stand together.

THE GAME OF WAR

In war men physically dominate over other men, visually vanquish a "foe." War is more interesting than chess - you get to play with real pawns. There are rules, strategies, advance and retreat, disappointment, elation and parades, and, best of all, camaraderie.

Not only, in war, can men exercise their bodies, release some of that testosterone, but they get to exercise their brain. They create bigger and better means to kill each other. At this point in history we rarely have hand-to-hand combat, we kill by remote weapons. We don't even know who we're killing, but we can tell it's a lot because the land is laid waste and on the news we see thousands of people starving and suffering - "collateral damage."

So now we know, through the news, that we're making "progress" in the war. Particularly in the Mid East where water is at a premium the tribes have developed exquisite means of torture to punish anyone who is thirsty and not a member of their specific group.

In the Mid East not only is torture "punishment," it's also exquisite entertainment.

Here in the "free" world war is big business, capitalism!, lots of profit, lots of important business and a two-martini lunch. The movie industry and the book publishers provide vast avenues for reasons, excuses, explanations, adventures and drama based on the game of war.

This titillate's the male ego.

When not at war, men are at football, rugby, hockey, basketball and chess, all substitutes for war, highly competitive, violent, rough, fun and a great outlet for aggression, frustration, and, camaraderie.

Over the years I have wondered what is the point of war. I can't find a logical reason. It's unnecessary. Nobody wins a war. I have told my students that, in a war, I kill a bunch of you…you kill a bunch of me… then back to I kill a bunch of you… you kill a bunch of me… - we're always at square one.

Of course the "answer" is "to vanquish the foe." What is a "foe" and how do we get one?

Who designs the choreography of war?

Men.

Who organizes war?

Men.

Who participates in war?

Men.

Who gets killed in a war?

Everyone.

The ostensible reason for war is to accumulate land, property for our "family," our tribe. We need ever more fertile lands and water for our population and more room for technical development.

As it stands today, we are short on pure water and short on farming.

Of course if leaders - religious leaders in particular, would allow us to control the increase in population, there is plenty of water and land at this point, to provide for everyone for millennia. But humane, intelligent birth control is not likely to happen. Many religions are hell-bent on over-population to rule the world.

And, to emphasize the need for "fodder," the churches, religious organizations who represent the "will of God," push for their followers to out-breed the competition - each other. It's another type of war - it's sick.

For example, the population of India at this time, 2018, is 1.35 billion people with a median annual income per person, $616.00. It is the poorest country with the highest population.

Indira Gandhi, Prime Minister of India (1966) instilled a program to reduce the poverty level and improve living conditions of the Indians; but it was cancelled after her untimely death. She focused mainly of reducing the monumental amount of unwanted children by the method of birth control. It was not well received.

It's not the life of a child that's important, what is important is fulfilling the whim of some religious leader who's goal is total $elf aggrandizement. And, we women, who are the "fall guys" accept this and support it.

And, we censor those of us who choose to think of the ramifications of unplanned births, concerned with the feelings and care of unwanted lives.

It seems to me that if we reduce the number of unwanted, unloved children, we'd have less need to kill off people for land. We might even have reason to get along, play nice.

Now, because we want "equality," we women want to join the incredible stupidity of slaughter. We want to fight beside our men in combat, to "take up arms" and vanquish the foe du jour.

We want to prove we're just as good as any man. Whatever he can do, I can do better! - or, at least close to that.

Do we actually want to prove we're as good as any man - or do we want to proceed, socially and economically in a more secure direction?

Oh, my. Again, incredible stupidity. We are NOT men. Never will be. Don't wanna be. Instead of emulating, aping, using men as a model, we should be what we are, creators of life, the monitors of intelligence, the teachers of, "All right, children - let's just get along; be nice and share."

Not a kind of Howdy Doodie, Charlie McCarthy, Pinocchio that echoes what our masters spout - the man pulls the string, and we speak.

Have women finally had enough? Will this attempt at "equality," respect, fade away - again, business as usual, for the next 40, 80 - 200, years?

THE SECRET MEANING OF SPORTS

For many years I assumed sports were a substitute for war; it's obvious… You have two sides and one goal. Two sides batter each other; one side out-runs, out-maneuvers, out-throws or out-distances the other side. For all this cleverness and brawn, you get a point.

But,

I have a cousin who is extraordinarily observant and thought - full. I was commenting that sports are a form of war.

Quietly she said, 'Carolyn, think about sports from a different point of view. In football, the men hug the ball, which is often placed between their legs. Then, to win the game, there is a designated area to "push," kick the ball through - the goal post.

The goal post has two "legs" spread apart so the ball can go through it. When a man forcefully gets the ball through the two, spread-apart posts - he "scores!"

Or the player can "hug" the ball and carry it himself to score.

In basket ball men "dribble" the ball - play with it, toy with it, up and down, across the floor. They vie with one another to get control of the ball, and when they do control the ball and get it into the "basket," they score!

???…interesting.

And, the cheerleaders cheer them on.

My cousin also pointed out the salary the cheerleaders get; the highest amount is *$150.00 per game,* or, *$3,500.00 per season.* It seems they're getting screwed.

AMERICA BEFORE WWII…A perfect world

Before World War II American home life was perfect - so said the TV shows and tradition.

Ask Donna Reed (The Donna Reed Show). She wore a tailored dress, pearls and heels to do the housework and the house was always perfect. Her husband Alex, a pediatrician, came home on time for dinner and their two sons were well-mannered and well-groomed. The family was courteous at all times; Donna, as the mother, never scolded her children that was the father's job. Alex listened to his children and counseled them - everything went smoothly. Children never talked back to their parents.

We were fed a carbon-copy daily diet of: "Father Knows Best," "I Love Lucy," "All In The Family," "The Adventures of Ozzie and Harriet," "Leave It To Beaver." "The Aldrich Family" and "George Burns and Gracie Allen," all palatable and predictable.

In my family, being Italians, we were loud, I guess. There was always food on the table, we had big meals of lots of stuff and almost always a few dirty dishes in the sink. Once, when a friend and I were leaving my house, she asked, "Why were you yelling at your mother?"

Yelling? At my mother? Surprised, I responded, "I wasn't yelling at my mother." That's the way we normally talk - over the top.

When I went to my friends' homes, the houses were so clean, no food out to grab a bite - the meals were planned; no leftovers in the refrigerators to hold you over to dinner. No one spoke much - it was so quiet. The father would listen to the news on the radio. Kids weren't allowed in the "parlor" while the father was home. He didn't like the noise.

Once a teenage boy came home and ate a loaf of bread before dinner. The mother was very upset. I didn't see a problem - he was hungry!

To me, the house was "empty," no signs or sounds of life…"bland" - in fact I just remembered a movie called, "The Blandings" and now I know what it meant - they were bland! Totally predictable!

Another girl friend, when we went to her house after school, she was hungry. She opened the refrigerator and there was a solitary package of cold hot dogs! We each had one. It was soooo good! At home I complained to my mother, "We never get cold hot dogs!" She said nothing.

The movies had cops and robbers; the "bad" guys died in the end and went to Hell. The love interest of the "good" guy had to be rescued under physically challenging conditions. In the climax, the two guys got into a fist fight, the bad guy holding a gun. The men would be fully entangled in a fight to the death with the heroine, always a blonde, cringing, in fearful anguish, pressed herself against the wall in some dark hallway.

In the fight, the "bad" guy's gun would be dropped close to the blonde's feet so she could easily reach down, pick it up and shoot the "bad" guy - but she never did! As a kid, about 7 years old, I would get so annoyed that she couldn't see how easy it would be to pick up the gun and shoot the "bad" guy!

Now I know it was a lesson to women not to be courageous, in charge, daring - that was the man's role. We're supposed to cringe - preferably against a wall - blonde.

Eventually, the "good" guy would stand up, unscathed, brush off his pants and the blonde would cling to her "savior." Without him, she was nothing.

Year after year, movie after movie, was built around this vacuous, predictable plot.

And, the interesting thing - unlike today's "entertainment," we all knew she had hips; she had mammary glands, legs, but they weren't on display to ensure we acknowledged them. She was nicely dressed and modest, and very feminine. In those days we took modesty as a sign of self respect.

On daily TV, the average family was depicted as: White, professional working father, stay-at-home Mom, four of the families mentioned had two sons or more, only one family had girls. Everyone was courteous and well-groomed.

Benign, wise, fathers, calm, indecisive mothers, respected each other, worked together, patience was the only emotion allowed.

That's it! No redress, no, "This stops here and now!"

Housewives supported each other; when there was a problem they acknowledge it by looking wise sending the message, "We understand." No discussion.

That was the American norm before the War, a perfect world.

WWII AND THE AFTERMATH

During the war years, 1941 - 1945, I was a kid in grammar school. Our time and lives were focused on "our boys" overseas - and, rightly so. We gladly did without all the comforts of life, butter, meat, shoes, tires and rubber erasers on pencils (in school I used erasers a lot!) but we were cooperating with the war effort. Our focus in America - all of us, concentrated on winning the war.

(FYI: The "rubber" erasers on pencils was some kind of black plastic. It made a black smudge on the paper when you "erased". The smudge was a reminder it was for the war effort.)

We and our allies won the war, at great cost. The "boys" - men, now, came home battered, traumatized, exhausted, subdued and angry.

Things weren't the same; although we all tried to get back to "normal," there was no "normal." Life was upside down.

Women had jobs; we had our own money to spend on extra stuff, conveniences, make-up, hats, shoes and lunches out. We didn't have to ask permission to buy something or, if we needed extra money, we didn't have to explain why.

We had cars and could drive. We women had built a life outside of home - we were drunk with the freedom and power in our lives. But we weren't satisfied. We wanted more. Some of us wanted a career and education - college. However, at that time very few women were admitted into higher education. Even then, professors assumed all we wanted were husbands (largely true). We were not taken seriously.

The men came home from the Pacific and Europe to be faced with a "war" on the home front. They had their jobs back, but not their life. The adjustment for the men was traumatic - they were frustrated. This was not the life they left - the life they expected to find when they came home; they felt abandoned; they'd gone to war, risked their life - for nothing! They come home to rebellious women.

Men wanted their "wives" back; the women who had worn a leash - a dog collar, who were required to "heel" when told to, were not obeying orders. Instead of preparing a home-cooked dinner, they were playing bridge and buying the new frozen foods for short-cut meals.

This idea of "home," was not what the men remembered; this was not the life they knew - or wanted. Men wanted tradition, "the way it was" before the war and women wanted freedom, a chance to breathe. We didn't want divorce, or leave the family, we just wanted more space to breathe.

It was a breakdown in communication.

As always, battered wives had no sanctuary. Traditionally a man had the right to control his wife any way he chose - what happened behind closed doors stayed behind closed doors. Occasionally there'd be a newspaper article about a wife who somehow got revenge on her husband's brutality. It would be written up as a comical piece about a husband who was too weak to control his wife; everyone would laugh at him. No mention of the wife's living situation or desperation was entertained for consideration.

The husband was King, ruler of his home. The wife's place was to obey and "make do." If the wife complained she was told to be a better wife; any dissension was her responsibility to correct.

Men were confused and frustrated.

We were frustrated too, but had no outlet.

Women had the vote, but that "right" fell far short of our needs. It was a long journey from 1870 to 1950.

WOMEN IN A TRADITIONALLY MALE ROLE

During the war, because all the trained, high-paid leaders of industry and society - the men - positions of responsibility and power, were handed over to women as a "loan," a stop-gap.

The supervisors, managers, leaders, directors, heads of departments and businesses were temporarily gone, off to war. This left great spaces in responsible, high-paying positions in white-collar businesses where women easily stepped in. The blue collar jobs, the ones based on physical adeptness, such as: Plumbers, car mechanics, riveters, welders, garbage "men," were also easily assumed by women.

Women were actively recruited to fill the jobs left by men. To assuage any distress of the men, they were assured that when they returned from the war, they'd get their jobs back.

In many cases, since women had never before been allowed positions of authority, the power of control - the sanction to "boss" others, went to their heads. We found our strength - we became invincible. We became bullies.

Physical strength took over for intellect; pushing, shoving and hitting just like men did; it didn't "solve" problems, but it gave women the feeling of power. Women had learned that men at times controlled their problems by slugging someone. So, women could do that, too. It takes no thinking or brain power to hit someone, but it can be effective to instill fear in people and create an illusion of respect for themselves.

The programs on TV, "entertainment," at that time were based on a general expectation and acceptance of abuse of women. When "Lucy" was spanked by her husband, "Desi," everyone laughed.

When Desi punished Lucy for some infraction of the house rules, he took away her monthly allowance. Everyone laughed.

In the movies all heroines were subject to control by men - women listened and obeyed. Music, "blues," "torch songs," were about women losing their man to another woman, but she loved him anyway, suffered in love, accepted abuse, understood that this was the place of the woman.

Song lyrics enforced the theme of male dominance:

"I'd even be glad just to be sad thinking of yooooo…some others I've seen might never be mean, might never be cross or try t' be boss, but they wouldn't dooooo; with all your faults, I love you still, it had to be you…" ("It Had To Be You." Billie Holiday.)

"Don't know why there's no sun up in the sky, Stormy weather, since my man and I ain't together, keeps rainin' all the tiiiime." ("Stormy Weather." - Lena Horne.)

"My Mama done tol' me, man is a two-face, a worrisome thing who'll leave ya ta sing the blooooo's in the night." ("The Blues in the Night" - Ella Fitzgerald.)

"I cried for you; now it's your turn to cry over me." ("I Cried for You" Frank Sinatra.)

"I remember every little thing you used to do, I'm so lonely,"("Lover Come Back To Me." Dinah Shore)

On Saturday afternoon, in the cowboy shows, the distressed woman was always rescued by the man in the white hat on the white horse: Hopalong Cassidy, Roy Rogers, The Lone Ranger or

Tom Mix. These were all ethical gentlemen - men we trusted and wanted to be like. - Oh, yes, they all sang and played guitar!

Up until WWII there we're no women "heroes." Women were "losers," and they were expected to accept loss gracefully and gratefully.

Because of the War our lives were turned upside down. Women had tasted freedom, and it tasted good - intoxicating.

IMPRESSIVE FEMALE HEROINES

History didn't leave women totally bereft of mention. We were humored with a few women who were noteworthy among the tattered pages of Time.

(60 c.e.) Boudicia The name of the English Queen **Boudicia**, is usually pronounced "boh dih SEE ah," but the spellings are varied (Boadicea, Boudicca, Boudica for a few) and the pronunciations also vary. But, after 2,000 years fly by, who remembers?

She was Queen of the Celtic Iceni tribe and lived, at that time, in Londinium (London). The Romans ruled England and decided to take over London as the final missing piece in their empire. But, this fiery red-headed queen thought otherwise.

On one attempt to subdue the Celtic queen they captured her, stripped her, whipped her in public and raped her two daughters. The women escaped from their cell.

Boudicia came back with a vengeance, attacked the Romans and lost. But, she set London on fire - burned it down; killed her two daughters and committed suicide.

For sheer ferocity and singled mindedness, Boudicia holds an honored place in English history. We could use her strength today!

(30 a.d.) Cleopatra, daughter of King Philip of Macedonia and sister to Alexander the Great, ruled Egypt which "prospered under Cleopatra". There were many Cleopatra's, it seems to have been a nom du jour in the royal circle - sort of like the Henry's, George's and Charles' in Europe.

She was a lively wench and had children by Mark Antony and Julius Caesar (among others), two of the greatest leaders of the time. She could hold her own as a clever, intelligent ruler, but after Mark Antony died by suicide she decided to end it all. No one knows for sure how she died, but it was suicide, probably bitten by an asp.

(1412) Joan of Arc, Jeanne d'Arc. France was at war with England, not doing too well. Joan, a teenager, heard voices tell her to fight for France. She was put at the head of an army and fought the English at the Battle of Orleans.

Jeanne was not intimidated by the sheer volume of men and the terror of war. She moved ahead and conquered the British army. France won the war, but later Jeanne was captured by the English and burned at the stake.

(1558) Queen Elizabeth I ascended the throne after Henry VIII died and England, according to history, prospered greatly under her rule. She ruled much of the Middle East, the British Isles and made great inroads into the islands south of the United States and also substantially influenced the settlement of America.

She died a normal death at 45 years old.

(1898) **Golda Meier** (Meir) Prime Minister of Israel 1969. She was a Zionist leader and helped create a Jewish state in Israel that the Jews consider their historical home.

As a child her family left the Ukraine for America to escape the terror of the murders of the Jews. She became an important political leader in forming and supporting the independence and modernization of Israel.

World leaders described her success as "she acts like a man," (Richard Nixon), and a tireless dedicated worker for all Israel.

(1917) **Indira Gandhi, "Iron Lady of India,"** the only female Prime Minister of India 1966 - 1984. As a "woman of Iron will" and ambition, she was a key architect of modern India.

Indira was ruthless; she ordered birth control for the general population and forced sterilization for impoverished males and people of "special needs" as we would say. She cleared the slums and jailed political opponents and activists. She was one of those rare people, of women in particular, who was a visionary for her country and made firm decisions.

She was assassinated. But her legacy is still one of strength and leadership as a model for women leaders.

Those women are not much different than we are. They had a destiny at birth that put them in a strong position to influence others - and they did influence thousands of people - still do.

In fact, being born to fame has a much stronger onus attached to it. If we're born with a "position," a place where we have great influence over others, our task then is to lift people up.

(1919) **Evita Peron** was chosen by destiny to be at the side of the President of Argentina, Juan Peron. Although the wife of the highest ranking citizen of a male-dominated society, Evita was a feminist and had schools and hospitals built, and created a welfare system for mothers. She also advocated suffrage for women in the 1940's (unsuccessful). She was far ahead of her time in the recesses of underdeveloped countries.

It is interesting to note that under the female leaders, all these countries prospered. Not one of them started a war and they took care of the needs of women. They got things done.

WOMEN BULLYING WOMEN

Sporadically, increasingly, women continue to slowly wake up and grow in strength and understanding. In the past few years, they've been protesting, demonstrating, striking out, complaining about bullying, sexual abuse, verbal insults, physical insults and other insidious problems - not just by men, but by other women!

There's been a crack in the dam of restraint for many years and now the dam has burst; frustration, anger, humiliation, anguish and pain are pouring out of much of the female American population, but, unfortunately, much of this is on each other. Women are used to being maligned so they're experts at using it on others.

And, other women are used to being hurt and used so they're not fighting back - they're hoping to sue. Suing may bring financial relief, but it's not the answer. The answer is to ferret out the cause of the bullying and correct it. Understanding a problem is the only way to find a solution.

But, often, they're focusing their anger on themselves. Who else is available? Women are used to being the underdog; we're used to being the butt of jokes, left holding the bag, stood up by, ridiculed by men and society.

Men laugh at our struggles for equality and few women support our cause for women's rights. We can't lash out at everyone to release anger. So who's left for us to vent our rage on?

Ourselves.

We are punishing each other for disrespecting each other. It's like hitting a mirror because the person looking back is ugly.

Now we're being "fat shamed" if we carry extra weight. We do it to ourselves; we shame ourselves.

> *On the news recently a "fat" young girl on a plane sat next to a young man who was texting his distaste at sitting next to her. She was reading the text over his shoulder and filming it for public display to show his disrespect toward her. Excuse me? Just who was showing bad taste? Him, for writing a private message to a friend, or her for snooping in his private "mail" and ratting him out to the world? He has **every right** to not like her; she has **NO right** to snoop in his private message. Who's the fool here? **She was shaming herself!** Then he was kind enough to apologize to her. She should apologize to him!*

Given this scenario, do we really think that men, and the overwhelming majority of conventional women will take us seriously? We don't take ourselves seriously, so, who else will?

If this young lady resents being labeled "fat," then why did *she* advertise it? *She* focused on it; *she* show-cased it; *she* "told" the world she was fat - he didn't! *She* made it public!

She doesn't understand the impact of her actions. If she had been sweet to him, she could have really shamed *him*! When someone hurts you and you gently show them where they "misunderstood" the situation, perhaps they'll understand there are better ways to react to unpleasant conditions.

Perhaps one way to handle "shame" would be, first, to keep your nose out of other people's correspondence. Secondly, if you feel so strongly about curtailing free thought and free speech, you might smile sweetly and say,

> "I'm sorry, I accidentally read your email and I guess you don't like sitting near me. But it'll only be for two hours. I hope we can be friends until we land in Montreal."

Who could resist liking you with that gentle, sincere approach? And, be slightly embarrassed at being so thoughtless to shame you? This is one of those moments where being a woman is a great advantage. You can use soft feminine wiles to show inner strength and win respect.

And, to end this discussion - and others like it, let's look at *the Truth*! I saw your post, young lady, and the TRUTH is: you are young, beautiful, healthy, intelligent and you have the spark of Life in your eyes - you are close to perfect!

This is what you should focus on, what you should see in the mirror. Look at the Truth of the gifts you have to share with the world. Don't waste your time trying to see what others see, far too many people need better eye glasses!

> *Once I got on a plane, tired and irritable. I sat next to a young man who was, apparently, tired and irritable also. He snarled at me for some reason, and I, not to be outdone, snarled back at him. After a short time, he leaned over and apologized for his rudeness, explaining he had just come from the funeral for his 18 year old daughter - she had been killed by her boyfriend. My heart melted. Through tears, I apologized.*

I think about this incident on occasion; it still hurts to realize how I could have said nothing in response, or, even apologized briefly for his discomfort (I don't recall what happened to make him angry).

But, no, I had to show him he wasn't going to disrespect me - I put him in his place!

But, no, what I actually did, was to put *myself in his place*; I stepped down to his level - I disrespected myself. I could have "turned the other cheek," or said nothing. That would have been so easy.

Then, when I understood the reason for his distress, I could have been of some comfort and lifted him up. For me, it was a painful lesson I'll always remember.

But, today, this is the immediate reaction all too often - "me good - you, bad." This is a sad state of our society, to immediately assume someone is the "enemy."

AFTERNOON ENTERTAINMENT

On the afternoon TV show, the two women - featured "guests" - are slugging it out in front of the TV cameras. Fists are flying, one women pulls at the hair of the other; the other latches on to a handful of hair at the scalp of the other. The two women kick, legs flying wildly at each others' shins and arms. Fists beat on each other's head and body. Loud, four-letter accusations of behavior and personal character burn the air.

Shrieking, swearing and yelling are loud, blunt weapons; each woman is determined to make the other one look bad, feel bad and get a broken nose in the process - "kill her dead" - a symbolic destruction of self.

The audience loves it. What the girls don't realize is that the two women engaged in rolling on the floor fighting, are symbols of how society perceives women; as "those who lower themselves to fight over a man. They have no shame, no respect, no standard of behavior."

The focus of this symbolic slaughter is Henry, who has been unfaithful to Eugenia - and Serenata, and Jolletta, and… It seems Henry had impregnated several young ladies when he was pledged to Eugenia - well, uhm, actually, she thought he was pledged only to her. So to right this redress, Eugenia was beating up her rivals to prove she was the only one allowed to benefit from Henry's charms.

Henry, the honoree, sat there, amid the melee, staring into the frenzied, unruly crowd, absentmindedly picking his nose, totally detached from the squalor in his honor. This appearance to his public is taxing and interferes with his nocturnal activities.

So goes the afternoon fodder for TV entertainment. Jerry Springer, Mauri Povich and Steve Wilko, among sundry other masters of titillation, lean back in their chair, laugh, and count the $$$. While the women roll on the floor making fools of themselves, the men sit back and count the profits. It's so easy - the women do all the wallowing and the men get all the glory, cash - and, respect.

The audience, composed of women, and men, revel in scatology, the lowest form of entertainment. It's so humiliating for anyone with a functioning brain cell to know this level of humanity exists.

How can we women demand respect from society when we don't respect ourselves? By bullying each other we women strive to assume the role of men, the leaders and power source at the head of society - the top dog. We assume the demeanor, the swagger, the privileges of men. But, we're not men.

You can't fool Mother Nature.

The end result of our behavior is to establish that we are not men, but we are women who behave like fools.

Women are becoming increasingly physical in their anger,; they're frustrated, speaking out, speaking honestly - as they see "honesty," eye-to-eye contact, loud voice, fists pumping the air, all a reaction to the seemingly, never ending humiliation from far too many sources.

Who are we impressing with this stupidity? Men? No, they see us as a joke - entertainment. Something rolling around on the ground, pulling hair, screaming, swearing; it's all for them, all about them - we want a man, we need a man - so we're told.

Any man of value would assume we're fools and head for the hills when they see us. A man with self respect wants a woman with the same values he has.

Think logically for a moment, to see a woman behaving like a wounded animal does not indicate behavior of value; it's cheap, available in any low-class group. Would anyone, any man, of any amount self-pride, want to associate with a person who rolls on a soiled floor, pulls hair and displays the intellect of a dead toad?

And, any woman of any amount of self-pride would not lower herself to this cheap behavior for attention and admiration.

But, but…here is the worst part (yes, the *worst!*)

The level of verbal barbs is somewhere in the neighborhood of wet Kleenex being thrown at you as a weapon.

One girl circles the other, eyeing her warily. "Henry really loves me - not you!"

The sharp-edged retort is immediate, "Oh, yeah?"

The volley is a sopping wet Kleenex, "Yeah." (o-o-o, that hurt!)

And so go the barbarous thrusts until the next commercial. Who can have respect for anyone who puts herself in this vacuous public arena?

No doubt there are those watching who think, "Hmmm, maybe we should rescind the right to vote…?"

If you want to go the mode of "barbarous thrusts," read 'Cyrano de Bergerac." Outside of William Buckley and Oscar Wilde, he is probably the main person with a ready wit and a quiver leaded with poisonous barbs.

THE BACHELORETTE

Programs like, "The Bachelorette," put a beautiful woman on the block, up for auction to some lucky man. The man needs no qualifications, any man will do - well, he has to be breathing, that's about it.

The bachelorette is one of 20 or so beauties who vie with each other for the longest eye lashes, the longest hair extensions, the smallest outfit tops and the briefest briefs to enhance their value in some man's opinion - in their "re-lay- shun ship."… Physical perfection is prized while moral or intellectual development is non extant - "I mean, like, like it's basically like, ama-a-azing." (smile here and stroke the silky extensions)

In essence they are "begging" for attention - groveling, competing - twiddling with their "For sale" sign, lowering the price and upping the stress level. So sad and so unnecessary.

By enhancing and displaying their body parts, these beauties are hoping to increase their value so that "he," "thee" man, Mr. Right, will choose the best of them - in his opinion - among the group. They will ride off into the sunset in a rented limousine for a month or so of sheer bliss. And then it's back to square one.

When men auction off steer, dairy cows, sheep - other critters - hogs - good health and good weight matter - in other words how good they look, I assume, is the major criteria. With the exception of false eye lashes and hair extensions women are judged on the same basis - how good they look.

How shallow.

Looking "good" in that sense is false, a mask, a character in a play that's like a "paper doll" - you play with it and then toss it out. When we get "tossed out," why are we surprised?

Did you know you get papers for the cattle when you buy them? These papers guarantee healthy animals.

You don't get papers at the "Bachelorette." Cows get more respect than the Bachelorettes do.

What woman, of any quality, of any self-respect, would put herself on display for ridicule, criticism and availability? It's a display of lack of self-pride, of cheapness, "going, going, gone!" for 6 weeks of pathetic, indiscriminate self-revelation, self-deprecation - a "ree-lay-shun-ship."

This is not "equality" - respect, it's just the opposite; it's humiliation, availability, cheapening.

Women support this behavior; women condone it; women attend it - need I go on? It's been 170 years since intelligent women put themselves on the line so you and I could have dignity and respect for ourselves.

But we continually work against lifting ourselves up out of the herd.

Do we really think #MeToo, NOW and the other women's crusades will have any lasting effect? Or is this another chorus in an old folk-tune?

RESIST NOT EVIL -

One of the major complaints of women in the workforce, women who are ambitious, is that often the males in leadership assume that these eager women will accommodate the men sexually in order to progress up the corporate ladder.

Probably it's not the expectation of sex specifically that is insulting to women, but the idea that, of course, women are available and eager to do anything to please. There seems to be a tacit agreement among the men that the women are a "sure thing."

That unspoken understanding is the insult.

But, the ensuing anger of the women is a part of the male entertainment - it just makes the women more desirable. That which you can't have is that which you covet. Men think, "If you say I can't have it, I'll make it a point to prove to you that I have the power, and you don't! I *can* have it! I *will* have it!'"

Being taken for granted and also being attacked will cause women to be angry and maybe cause retribution. Both of these actions give "power" to the men. They have our attention and energy no matter under what conditions. Anger and Retribution are forms of "love," of attention, a reward - we dance to their tune.

I'm going to suggest a completely opposite reaction to an insult. Opposite, and I believe, very effective.

From the Bible, Book of Matthew, Chapter 5, verses 39 - 44 tells us not to resist evil; if someone slaps you, give him the other cheek. It goes on to say to love your enemies, bless people who hate you and curse you; pray for people who use you badly.

I've had a really hard time with this. How can you teach people you're serious, you mean business - respect you, when they won't leave you alone? How can you demand respect when someone is pawing you and has you pinned to the desk? One good smack in the right place at the right time can send an impressive message to someone to shape up - or else!

Let's suppose that after being insulted, lied to and cheated you sue someone, and win. Suppose you manage to disgrace them, humiliate them and grind them to dust.

Does this make you happy?

The young women who are molested or impregnated by famous politicians, actors and CEO's can get a good price for the story from pulp magazines and they can get featured in the news. Yes, these men can be dragged down, lose their livelihood and family.

But, what does it say about the women? They can extract revenge for dastardly deeds in a far more devastating way - by kindness.

When you sue in public, demean someone in public, drag their name in the dirt, your anger, pain, you bring yourself down there with them - in the dirt.

That is "resisting evil." You shame yourself in order to shame someone else.

To deal with evil is by rising above it; not responding, not feeding it energy.

You are badly treated, you hire a bull-dog attorney and sue. Let the attorney handle it all. Every inch of you is a lady; you don't get your hands dirty, and, oh, you are so believable! Everyone will admire you - even the Chairlady of the Vestry at Grace Cathedral- the ultimate in conservatives!

This is how you win. Rise above it. This is how your "enemy" is disgraced - he'll do it to himself!

Sue, by all means, but don't wallow in insults or, "he did… she did…" Get redress, revenge by circuitous means; by that I mean legally and without looking back. Men all too often are sore losers. But, they'll get over it. Actually, I'm happy to share anything as long as I get half - that's enough for me.

RELIGION

Women's Lib is often seen as going against the Word of God. According to the source, the Bible, women were created as a Helpmeet to men. The man's status is just below God and women are just below the man. Therefore, men are, spiritually, above us, so by default, "above" us in every part of life.

Just before this edict it is written that Eve ate the fruit because the serpent enticed her. When Adam ate the fruit, he ate it of his own free will. Why is that Eve's fault?

Apparently that position, that status - men being under God, means women should be humiliated, beaten, degraded, forced to bear children in "pain," because Eve was lied to - the serpent led her to trust him; she was pure-minded. But Adam exercised his free will in disobeying God…

And, when Eve told Adam to "eat of this fruit," he could have said, "No, thanks, Eve not a good idea." And perhaps, pled her case of ignorance, innocence, in her behalf before God. You know, be a man!

Instead when God asked, "Who ate of this fruit?" Adam pointed to Eve and said, "She made me do it!"

To this day men blame women for what the man does wrong - it not his fault; it's hers.

Enough of stupidity!!

And, think about it, Eve was the size of a rib, what, maybe 15 inches or so big? How could she put a 1/2 Nelson on Adam to force the apple down his throat?

There are men, mortal men, who have created a religion in which they become God, (yes! God!) after they die! In this life their wives and daughters are exhorted to obey them, "be sweet," because the females are talking to "God."

How can women gain respect when we are faced with that fatuous logic? When we die, we go directly to dust, but when men die, they go directly to "always was and always will be."

How can that be?

Keep thinking! The people in this same belief say they "have" the "One True God." If, when they die, each man becomes God, how, then, can there be "one" god, and which one is the True One?

Yes, I hear there are "false" gods, but how do you know which are the false ones?

Is that blatant male aggrandizement?

Are there other people who find this concept incredibly vacuous?

In some religions, the priest or pastor's duty is to intervene for God - he stands between you and God. *You* can't pray directly to God you have to go through a channeler, an interpreter, a screener. It's ok to pray to saints - they'll get the word to God. But, many of the saints are women.

It's all so confusing.

> *At church there was a man who said (adamantly), "I take the Word of God verbatim!" "Verbatim?" I thought. "That's impossible!" So I challenged him to a "verbatim" duel. In the church office, we sat, facing each other. He started, "Now in the Book of Genesis, God said... Now, what that means is..." At the point he said, "...what that **means** is..." I shouted, "NO! NOT what it 'means' - we're doing this verbatim!" He continued, "But, what it means is..." I bellered, "NO! NOT "means"! **VERBATIM!**" It went downhill from there. Then, I remembered he was an engineer - they don't do "words" - they do weights and measures. I got up and left.*

Ironically, if God is our "Father,", shouldn't we *all* be "proud?" Shouldn't we seek to raise up the perception of *each* child? If God created females and He loves us, shouldn't we be treated with respect - treat *everyone* with respect?

Isn't the "**ONE** Great Law" an admonishment and guide for *all of us*?

Matthew 22:36-40 King James Version

The One Great Law is:

Thou shalt love the Lord thy God with all thy heart, and with all thy soul, and with all thy mind.

and, the second part of the One Great Law is:

80

And, Thou shalt love thy *neighbor as thyself.*

On these two commandments hang all the law and the prophets.

Are our "neighbors" men *and* women?

I'm confused, as usual. This commandment is inclusive, carte blanche for everyone to be respected. Why then, do men usurp God's commandment and put themselves closer God than they do women? It seems we're equally due respect.

And, another point that confuses me is I've been told, "God wrote the Bible." Other people tell me "Scribes wrote the Bible." If God's word is infallible, it's understandable that we take it verbatim.

But, if it's done by scribes, who dictated it? Did the scribes ever goof off, nod at their work? Stay too long at the toilet, miss some information..? There are so many contradictions - even though people excuse them away…

For example, if only Adam and Eve existed in Eden and they had two sons, one killed the other - Cain killed Abel, then there were only 3 people on earth. But, Cain went to Nod, a place near Eden and got married.

He married who? (whom?) How did she get there? Something is haywire; I'm missing a big piece of information right at the start. I asked this question of someone who is a Fundamentalist, the Bible is the Word of God, and she said, "It took time."

…? Time? I don't follow. Was Cain's wife a time traveler?

Do we all agree there is but one God? Is God a *man* who walked with Enoch? Or, is God a *spirit*? Is it true *gods* married the daughters of man?…"God…**s**"…?

And what about the plea Jesus made while he was on the cross? He said, "My God, my God, why have you forsaken me?" "*MY*? God?" Why not just, "God! God! Why have you forsaken me?" Is Jesus from a specific "mansion" in heaven?

Perhaps one day we'll know. Until then, we have the One Great Law to guide us.

The point I'm making is that if there is some confusion about the initial data in the records, perhaps there is confusion in other places. For instance the very low level of respect for women:

> They have to keep their hair covered because if they don't a man will get an erection at prayers and that's her fault. Women must bear children in pain to punish Eve because Adam bit the apple. Well, she *did* bite the apple - *but so did Adam*. What's *his* punishment? Women should keep quiet in church. A woman is below her husband in importance.

As to the people who believe this is Truth, a direct line from God, do they know the world isn't flat?

Today we complain about the skewed, slanted information in the history books. Is it possible the Old Testament has some misunderstandings, some garbled information, some slanted data also. Is it possible we could understand the goodness and greatness of this ancient information source and still see each other, men and women, as equal in value? I understand that in ancient texts words and symbols often have several meanings. Do we *know* the translations are accurate?

Leonard Schlain, author of "The Alphabet vs the Goddess," was a neurologist and part-time archeologist . On his digs he collected goddesses from ancient civilizations but then realized that at a certain point in civilization goddesses disappeared and male gods took over.

He theorized that the linear script of the Arabs gave men the strength and motivation to dominate women goddesses and took over the reins of civilization. Apparently the brain's neural construction facilitates the male cognitive operation - men think linearly and women think vertically.

Also with the advent of linear script, there was an increase of war and domination of weaker peoples. Linear script is "doing" and vertical thinking is "feeling."

The book, "The Alphabet vs the Goddess," is a compelling read into the erosion of civilization by female subjugation. The impetus for the change was the alphabet, linear thinking which is a male attribute (engineers).

It is interesting that in ancient religions, the gods were part male and female - each half of the other. In Egypt, the leader, the Pharaoh was half male and half female. The Pharaoh wore a fake beard as the designation of leadership.

JESUS AND HIS RELATIONSHIP TO WOMEN

On the Sundays at the Milpitas jail for women, when I gave the talks, the congregation was about 1/2 black women and 1/2 white women. They were incarcerated for prostitution or selling drugs - to support their boyfriends.

Most of them were mothers with their children farmed out here and there; women and girls who had no concept of self- respect. They were raised in an environment where their reason-to-be was to obey a man and please him. It was a life of limited choice, egregious disrespect.

At the jail, I often used the behavior of Jesus in his interaction with women as an example of how a man should treat a woman:

First of all was his mother; he held her in very high esteem. They both knew of his ability to perform miracles. At the wedding in Cana the host ran out of wine.

Jesus' mother asked him to please take care of the problem and he replied something like, "Well, I'm not supposed to be doing that yet." But, hey, he's a good Jewish son - so he turned water into wine. No way would he refuse his mother.

He met the Samaritan woman at the well and asked for a drink of water. The woman was hesitant because he was a Jew and she a Samaritan who were considered low class people. But Jesus reassured her that she was a worthy person; he held her in esteem. He drank the water she offered him.

An adulteress was supposed to die because she was caught having sex with someone other than her husband. Because she broke the law she was condemned to be stoned to death. Jesus told the accusers if anyone of them was blameless, then they should caste the first stone. Everyone left - no one caste a stone.

A woman who had been menstruating for many years went to Jesus to be healed. She dared to touch the hem of his garment and then her faith healed her. At that time women were not allowed to touch a man they didn't know. Jesus knew he had been touched by a stranger. He spoke kindly to her and said it was her faith that healed her, not him.

Usually in society, if a person is high-ranking, he or she is given the privilege of being first for some special honor. If a new library is built in town, probably the Mayor or someone of distinction has the honor of cutting the ribbon to open the doors for everyone else.

In the life of Jesus, as related in the Bible, women were the first to know about the major events of Jesus.

The first to know he was arriving was Mary, his mother-to-be. Then the second was her cousin Elizabeth who knew by intuition that Mary's child would be exceptional.

At the end of his mortal life, when Jesus arose and left the tomb, three Mary's were there to see the miracle, his mother Mary, Mary Magdalene and another Mary who was not stipulated. There were several Mary's who interacted with Jesus at that time.

These three women had the honor of seeing him just after he assumed his immortal form. And two women were the first to know when he was coming.

All through his life, Jesus showed great respect to women. *Everyone* should all follow that example.

We should all respect ourself first and then all others. This lifts everyone up to know how valuable we are, how gifted we are, each in our own way.

I happened to turn on PBS in the middle of a documentary about a tribe in the Middle East. I don't know what tribe it was but the people were extraordinarily beautiful. The women had very long hair, black with soft waves; they were slender, lithe. The men all had beards and mustaches as is common in the Middle East.

They had gorgeous, large almond-shaped eyes, slender nose, high cheek bones - really breathtakingly beautiful.

The announcer said, "This is probably the tribe Jesus came from."

That caught me by a pleasant surprise. I thought, "Of course! Jesus must have been beautiful. For the son of a carpenter to hold thousands of people enthralled by his words, his deeds and his personality, there, also, must have been something beautiful for them to see."

And we all know that kindness, agape, has its own beauty.

As an aside, the name, "Mary," means "stubborn" in Hebrew. I can't imagine why anyone would name her child "Stubborn." Perhaps "Steadfast" would be a better interpretation.

MARRIAGE

In the sitcom "Modern Marriage," the mother, "Claire," has a day off of "mothering" the family. She has arranged her schedule so she has a block of "her" time - some space, silence, freedom from family pressure to spend at her leisure.

She picks up a book to read and says to the TV audience, "At last I have a quiet afternoon I can be in peace; all I want to do is sit and read, quietly."

In comes her husband, sits next to her and wants to talk. She looks balefully at the TV audience - there goes her time of leisure, her private time to enjoy herself.

The idea of marriage was created long before the concept of Christianity was inserted in the contract. It crafted the union of two people into a binding, life-long association. Around the 1100's the concept of the "contract" was designed for men to ensure that their property went to selected offsprings after the death of the chieftain or tribal head.

Marriage had nothing to with a woman being a "helpmeet" at that time; it was a matter of property, ownership and legacy. Ownership of "property" had nothing to do with "God." That is a fairly recent coda to the ownership contract of marriage. If God is inserted in the concept of a legal union, then marriage becomes "supernatural," a superstition; if you break your marriage vows God will punish you.

Just recently the words, "honor and obey" in the woman's contract, were removed from the traditional wedding vows. Many engaged people write their own contracts today; they say what's meaningful to them.

Therefore the concept of a woman being "under" the domination of a man is invalid. Yes, women are smaller, usually, and weaker - physically. But equal in their importance to society. After all, Eve was the size of a rib and look at the impact she had on the future of Life!

Some women define marriage for women as "a life of your own." This perception is typical of the narrow, limited thinking of many women. One of my friends was married to an alcoholic. In her world, marriage was security, a predictable, comfortable life. The definition of "a life of her own," meant spending countless nights preparing dinner for a man who came home hours late, dead drunk, threw up and passed out on the couch. That is not a "life of **my** own," that is Hell.

> *Think of the symbolism of "marriage." This "joining" together was a contract created by men. God had nothing to do with it. Marriage is the symbolic slaughter of the enemy - woman. A virgin dressed in white designates purity at the time of her sacrifice. She makes a promise to be faithful, puts on the symbol, brand, of ownership, the ring. It's only fairly recently men have rings. Her name is changed, her identity is removed, "Gladys von Hefflbaum" dies at the altar and*

If a woman enjoys being a "helpmeet," fine. However, Khalil Gibran defines marriage as being two trees who stand side by side, not in each others shadow, but together to share Life. He advises not to drink from each other's cup but to be sure that each other has a full cup. This "caring" is the ultimate act of love.

At times, helping someone too much, is not "love," it's crippling them. The person becomes dependent, helpless, useless to him/her self. We need to teach self-reliance, understanding of an issue, how to intelligently change, control or adjust to an issue. This is "maturity," not dependence.

It's not standing "alone," we stand by inner strength. We don't let anyone carry us; we don't lean on anyone; we walk side by side.

His definition of marriage, then, is a union of respect; two adults who appreciate sharing, helping and the full enjoyment of being with each other.

MANIPULATION - BUSINESS AS USU-AL

When I taught Communication classes, in the first class I would announce, "Class, I'm going to teach you to lie, cheat and manipulate people. Why would I do that?"

Often the reply would be, "Because that's how you win, how you get ahead."

"No, that's not why."

But, often a student would say, "Because that's what people do to you."

"Exactly! *That's what people do to you!* But, I don't want you, to ever, do that to others - you don't need to. Don't lower yourself. You can 'win' by honesty, by being truthful and sleep well."

Then, I'd teach the rhetoric of lies. Everyone, not just girls, needs to know the ways they're manipulated in politics, life situations and partnerships.

Don't trust anyone. Think for yourself.

To learn to do this takes maturity, the ability to separate needs from wants. It takes understanding, analysis, to weigh consequences, and perhaps there is some degree of sacrifice. Thinking for yourself can be a lonely, scary process, but it can be ultimately rewarding in independence and inner strength.

INCEL Involuntary Celibates

People assume the women's movement is a hate-men group. No, it's not. It's a leave-me-alone movement, a don't-annoy-me movement, a give-me-some-respect movement, a give-me-some-space movement.

We are not isolationists nor frigid, nor bitter. We really like most people, nice people, men - anyone who wants to play fair.

But, there are men who have created a group called "InCel," Involuntary Celibates (incidentally the title was a woman's idea.)

These men are not "celibate," by choice; they can't get women to have sex with them, so they're "involuntarily celibate."

These men are extremely - perhaps pathologically - angry because they are not able to entice women, or attract women into having sex with them. They hold the women responsible because these men can't exert their "manhood" and procreate or just enjoy the moment - relieve sexual tension.

Please note, it isn't "companionship" these men want, it's sex, plain old sex - no fancy shmancy ritual, (flowers, wine, dinner) just sex. And, they can't entice women to see their point of view!

So, to even the score, the men kill women. There have been incidences of men who, in a fury of hate-women mode, run down groups of people walking on a sidewalk, attempting to kill as many women in the group as possible.

I fail to see how killing women will fix their problem; the more women they kill the fewer there are to have sex with them - the men are working against themselves. There is always the very definite possibility some woman will find this bizarre attitude as "manly strength" and fall over backward to fulfill an empty ego.

The men are described as rough, insulting, demeaning, selfish, hateful - just gather all the characteristics that are despicable and apply them here. And with this ugly approach to life these men feel entitled to sex by any woman of their choice.

Amazingly, many women do not find this attitude and behavior attractive.

And I say "amazing" because I know *so many* women who are hungry for a man - *any man.* This is the sole thrust of their conversation, men, where are they, where is "the one" for me, how do I look? Will I attract some man? I'm getting plastic surgery to look younger for a man, bigger breasts (one's breasts cannot be big enough to attract a man, is their consensus. Unfortunately, much of the time this is true - pathetic.)

(In discussing the meager bathing apparel of many young women and the scarcity of the material in blouses for the same young ladies, thus revealing the totality of their mammary glands, I asked the boys in one of my classes, "Don't you ever get tired of seeing the same thing all the time? Do you ever say, "Oh, I've already seen that!" They burst out laughing and said, "That'll never happen!!" Pathetic.)

From my perspective, a huge population of women are laying for, hunting for, plotting for - obsessed with, hunger for, need, desire for, a man - "a" man, *any man* will do. (And I laugh at the boys!)

One of my friends, a woman in her 70's was so desperate for a man she actually had sex with the apartment house janitor - on the floor of the elevator.

Now, sex with the janitor is not the problem - it's the cold, hard floor of the elevator at her age of 70+.

That's what I mean by "desperate!"

(I hope he had vacuumed the floor first.)

These warped personalities will not support any women's liberation movement as those women who are desperate for approval and acceptance by men cannot understand that the perception of "panic" is diametrically opposed to self-respect.

Can you believe, there are these men who can't get a woman?

Ken, a man at my church hated women and took every opportunity to say so. My church was a group of elite intellectual Leftists (not me!) who made allowances for all types of aberrant behaviors (me). Ken was divorced and loudly, constantly lamented the fact that his wife got a job and became independent. Ken advocated rescinding suffrage for women and not allowing them to work. He was serious!

Ken also went on solitary mountain treks to be alone and commune with God.

On one occasion many of us were in the church kitchen preparing a communal meal when Ken put his knife down and said, "God spoke t'me, and God said..." and went on with something about God hating women.

I had had it! I put my knife down and said, "God spoke t'me, too and she said, 'Carol, don't listen t' Ken, he's full'a shit.'" All the ladies put their head down and smiled. The men looked confused.

LGBTQ Lesbians, Gay, Bisexual, Transgender, Queer

Today it seems people need to proclaim their sexual preferences loudly by banners, titles, parades and dramatic modes of apparel. This information is "overload" for the average person.

Are you at all interested in someone's sexual preference? Why should anyone be interested in yours?

Recently I was shopping in a craft store. There was a customer who drew everyone's attention, nice dress, sweet smile, cute shoes and bag, lucky to have naturally curly hair. Except for his beard and mustache he was quite pretty.

The basic premise of this movement is to remove the focus on gender differences. We are not our gender. We are not our skin color. We are souls, beings of great intelligence and creativity designed to help each other on this planet.

A young mother was showing off her new-born son to the neighbors. We were all looking, admiring and loving the little guy. An older neighbor woman came up, seeming very concerned about the baby. With great urgency she asked, "What is it?!"

The mother replied, "A boy." Greatly relieved, the woman said, "Thank God!"

I couldn't help it. I gave her a rather curious look as to why she'd ask that question. It seemed to me the better question should be, "How are the mother and child doing? Are they fine?"

Then maybe ask what is the gender.

But…this group of Alternative Gender people is leveling the playing field; the message seems to be, "Gender isn't important - the person is."

They're obliterating "differences." What people do behind closed doors is no one else' business. They call attention to their right to be who they choose to be and they support each other.

Heterosexual women do not support each other; we don't have solidarity. President Trump stepped into the Brett Kavanaugh fracas and was crass enough to ridicule the nightmare of Christine Ford's (alleged) sexual attack by Kavanaugh.

The women in the audience laughed loudly and clapped at Trump's portrayal of Dr. Ford's trauma. Laugh? - at someone's pain? It's sick. It so easily could happen to them and they would be faced with carrying the nightmare, alone, for decades as victims of rape do.

Recently Melania Trump, First Lady, spoke out about the trauma of Dr. Christine Ford's alleged rape by Brett Kavanaugh. Melania sagely suggested that in the future if we cry rape, we should have proof.

I totally agree. Next time I go to Trader Joe's to buy Cheerioats, I'll take a rape kit along. I can see why Trump chose her to wed. They have so much in common.

People ask about rape, "Why didn't you report it?" How can you adequately verbalize a nightmare, a terror? Just hearing the words brings back the fear, the helplessness of the act, the event. Who want to relive that moment, over and over; who can ***prove*** how degrading it is, how damaging to the human soul?

But the Alternative Life Style community supports each other. They take the time to listen and understand. Even in the off-norm sexual preference population, they support each other. Good for them.

When California had Proposition 8 on the ballot, dis-allowing same-sex marriage, the proposition was worded in such a way that if you voted "Yes," you voted against it. The wording was deliberately tricky. It was designed by same-sex marriage opponents; if you said, "No," you voted for it.

People in Utah sent in millions of dollars to support the Proposition and there were many protests and physical demonstrations for it - against same-sex marriage. Tricky!

Groups of women crowded street corners waving bright signs supporting the Proposition. Their beautiful, blonde, blue-eyed children crowded around them, all smiling and bobbing up and down. The women smiled and clapped their hands as people drove by.

The message on the signs indicated that if same-sex people married, they couldn't have children. The message was so obviously stupid I had a hard time thinking the women were serious.

The message suggested that if same-sex people marry, they can't/won't have children. So, then, I ask, "If same-sex people marry they won't have children. And if same-sex people don't marry, will they STILL not have children?"

Ultimately, whether they marry or not, they won't have children. It doesn't make any difference. And, if they want children, they can adopt. You can adopt a child of any race, size and gender to meet any needs.

The fact is that there are couples who can't have children and older people who are lonely marry for companionship. Being happy and making someone's life a joy should be the main goal of marriage.

Kim Davis, the Kentucky Marriage License Clerk refused to give a marriage license to a gay couple who were exercising their legal rights by applying to get married. Kim said her religion forbid the marriage of two people of the same sex.

What Kim doesn't understand is, there is a separation of church and state in America. She had no legal right to refuse the two men a marriage license. She was praised by her community for denying the gay couple their right to "pursue happiness." Across the nation people of the Alternative Life Style came to the defense of the gay couple.

The Alternative Life Style community tries to understand, guide and support their community. They don't split into opposite groups. They help each other.

Kim should have been fired.

There are American Indian tribes that revere and support homosexuality. In the Cherokee Nation often a "man/woman" is a respected member of the tribe and is a type of seer or psychologist to help settle personal problems.

The man may be in woman's attire as a general outfit and this is considered appropriate for his title. There is no stigma attached to gender preference and he's fully accepted for who he is.

One Cherokee brought up the point that today, the title, "Native Americans" is a gross fallacy as before the pilgrims arrived there was no "America." The explorers referred to this big chunk of land as, Novas Modus - "New World."

The Far Left group of today should refer back to history, learn it, then ask today's indigenous people how they feel about what to call them. The Far Left is grossly out of line, masters of unilateral didactic, vacuous decisions.

It's well known the ancient Greeks were relaxed in their sexual preferences and sexual activities. But, aren't we all…

Today we might see some of their sexual practices as unhealthy, physically and psychologically damaging. But the point is, gender preference in sexual activities or partnerships is a personal choice. We've all seen heterosexual couples where we wonder, "What on earth does she see in him (or her)."

Who cares?

I knew one couple, very much in love, been married many years and had two grown sons.

The man, a retired Naval Captain was a slight, thin, balding man. His wife and sons were quite tall and weighed well over 300 lbs each.

The man was bemoaning the fact that since he retired from the Navy, he couldn't find a job.

It was killing me to restrain from saying, "Well, you could hook up your wife and sons to plow the north forty." He could make a million hiring them out to AAA for towing.

I'd never make it as a psychiatrist.

People assume the women's movement is a hate-men group. No, it's not. It's a leave-me-alone movement, a don't-annoy-me movement, a give me respect movement.

Respect is the magic word. But…

Prostitution should be legal, we should have businesses where women will allow themselves to be raped, ravished by men who feel forcing themselves on women will make them more "manly" - more successful…?

The girls could charge double… triple? Think of their income tax…we could pay off the national debt.

THE TROUBLE WITH SONS IS THEIR MOTHER

One of my close friends has 3 sons and one daughter. For some reason one day we were discussing her children and she said, "The trouble with sons is their mother."

I gave that comment a lot of thought. In my family of cousins, all the sons were chosen first for any treat and were spoken to in great reverence. We girls were well-treated, but not as good as the boys. It didn't seem right to me. I never mentioned it at the time - didn't seem like a good idea.

For example, two of my cousins, brother and sister, came home to lunch from school. The boy was about 6, the girl 8. The boy was fed in the house at the table, the girl was fed out on the porch steps.

She mentioned this to me when she was in her 40's - she was still fuming; it hurt so bad. I couldn't understand fully at the time what she was saying - it was so wrong. I could go on with a litany of mistreatment, blatant inequities of how girls are treated in homes. But it's pointless. And, yes, in many cases boys are badly treated, too. What gain is there by mistreating children? What does that teach them?

Either way this breaks my heart.

In China the girls are "allowed" to die in their cribs. Recently in San Francisco a group of Chinese officials held a convention to discuss the lack of girls available to marry the boys. The boys were 2:1 more in the population. What is there to discuss at a convention? If they had a handy abacus these officials could easily see, if you kill off 50% of something, then you have 50% less!

In the Mid East the treatment of females is despicable. God help the women there.

Here, in America, women have more rights than anywhere else in the world. But, in the southern states and the states where religion is strong, women's rights and respect for women are grievously limited.

One difference between America and other countries is, we lie about how we respect women. We're told we women get better pay, better living conditions and better treatment than anywhere else.

And, we do.

But, we're still below the mark in America where women are valued for what they contribute to society. We're still regulated to underdog status; we get a pat on the head instead of a raise if we behave well. It's humiliating, but we grit our teeth and put up with it.

One of my friends, another Communication Studies Instructor, was musing about her son. As an off-hand remark she asked, "I wonder what my son really thinks of me."

I said, "Let's find out."

We created a form where we asked 40 young men, college students, "What do you really think of your mother?"

The overwhelming response was that boys liked their mother - but - the one response that we were completely unprepared for was,

"I just wish she would stand up for herself more often."

*"**Stand up for herself** more often"*!

We were stunned! What a volume of covert information that says about her, him, and the family dynamics!

MANNERS

British actor, "Superman," Henry Cavill expressed his confusion in asking a girl for a date. He said, "It's difficult to date if there are certain rules in place…" meaning what are the rules today?

Yes, there are "rules" - they're called "MANNERS," an antiquated custom predating, "If it feels good, do it." For those of you born - indoors - after 1960, let me explain what "manners" are.

They are a set of behaviors designed to show the other party respect. You show an appreciation of, or a recognition of their presence, or their presents - as the case may be.

This is done, by returning phone messages, answering written invitations by phone or in writing, showing up **on time** for engagements, not interrupting others in their discourse - unless the house is on fire - and so on.

In conversation, you speak and then, listen, to the incoming message bytes. If you are asking for a date, you actually use the words that indicate, "This is a request to spend some time with you." Be *specific* in your message.

For example a man in the church choir asked me, "Are you going to the concert?"

"Thee" concert...? I didn't know the church choir was attending a concert...

I said, "I don't know..." I assumed perhaps he was arranging group transportation.

He said, "Let me know as soon as possible."

I forgot about it. Weeks later I realized he was asking for date and I didn't pick up on that. But, here's the punch line, his wife had just died and he was saddled with four small children to care for. He saw me (a single woman) as a candidate for the job of picking up where his wife left off.

He married his au pair. I dodged a bullet.

When you ask your *specific* question, "Can you come over to dinner on Tuesday?"

"I have two tickets to the Smashing Lightbulbs Concert, would you like to go?" and if the other person says, "I don't know…," or "No, thanks." Take this as a "NO." Don't pursue it. Don't ask them again.

Some people have a really hard time hearing, "No." If when you ask someone for a date and they appear "dodgy - hesitant," take that as a "No" and let go of it.

At one company-required meeting we had to choose partners. I didn't know anyone there so I asked a young man seated next to me if he'd be my partner. He snorted and walked away. I took that as a "No."

Send "Thank you" notes, *always* acknowledge a gift, a favor - any out-of-the way deed with a "thank you," sincerely meant. Send your thanks by email, smoke signals, carrier pigeon - whatever…

Over time I sent my grandchildren various gifts - never got a "Thank you." I sent each one a bundle of "Thank you" notes, stamped and addressed to me. Never got one back. I sent one college student $1,000 to help with expenses - no "thank you, at all! Well, it'll save me writing checks in the future.

If you're at a bar and you see someone you'd like to meet, go up to the person, smile, and ask, "Hi. I'm Joe (you can insert your own name here.) I'd like to get to know you…" Don't *ever* put your hands on *anyone* unless they ask for help.

No, Henry, the rules haven't changed, they're just covered in cobwebs. Oh, I almost forgot, for heaven's sake put your hand over your mouth if you sneeze or cough. Try to sneeze or cough into the corner of your elbow - if you have time. **DO NOT: Pick your teeth, floss your teeth, pick your nose, clean your ears or <u>yawn</u>, in public!** (In some cultures this is acceptable - it is <u>*NOT*</u> acceptable in America.)

101

I was shopping at one of those huge discount stores when a woman walked by, yawning a full open-mouth yawn. I was terrified I'd fall into her mouth - I hung on to my cart! It was *disgusting!*

You'll always be safe with: Please, Thank you, Yes thank you, No thank you, and for you girls, you can always say, "**NO!**" and sign up for karate.

In particular, when you're talking and someone keeps interrupting you, it's a sign of what low esteem they have for you. You can't fight it; the more you object, the more they control you. You can either: be totally silent, refuse to talk, or just keep talking over them. If they have no respect for you, you have to have respect for yourself.

Girls, **never go alone** to a man's apartment, unless you want to… (fill in the blanks). It sends a lot of messages about you and the value of yourself. If you want to meet someone for lunch, coffee, meet them at a designated place, *always meet around other people. Bring your own transportation.*

Never let any man, or woman, you don't know into your apartment when you're alone. If someone you don't know well stops by "for a minute" and needs to use the phone - the bathroom - get drink of water, then bring the phone, water out on the porch. Plumber is due at the bathroom - sorry, not working.

I held classes in manners for children ages 9 -12. We talked about dining, what fork to use, proper attire for what occasion, small talk, appropriate topics, serving meals, cutting a cake, eat with your mouth closed… only girls came.

FATHER - DAUGHTER INCEST

In the '70's I did a paper on prostitution and discovered that a great percentage of young prostitutes were run-aways from their homes. The girls were seeking asylum on the streets - a place safer for them than home.

They were running away from their fathers. These men, touted, lauded as care-givers, family men, churchgoers and responsible citizens, were a source of terror for the girls; home was not a safe place for them.

The data I found at that time was that 7 out of 10 of ***reported cases*** where fathers molested their daughters.

Hard to believe. Impossible to accept.

I couldn't find any graphs or hard data on the subject (2018). There were very few articles and some studies that touched lightly on the subject.

If 7 out of 10 is an even remotely accurate number of fathers molesting their daughters, why is the number so high? Where are the mothers? Why isn't this addressed in the courts, in the home, in the press - in the Supreme Court? By the Law of Averages, heinous crimes will always happen - but 7 out of 10? *Forever?*

"It's a he said she said." Unacceptable! Yes, physical evidence is critical, evidence, proof, but in many cases "proof" is inaccessible. Is it possible we could use lie detector results as an *indication* of a "possibility?" - maybe not real "proof" but an indication?

I suspect that this behavior of fathers is considered so abhorrent and ugly that researchers are reluctant to advertise it in any data with public access.

Or, they're covering up for each other.

Tarana Burke talks about a girl who shared her story of being molested by her stepfather; she told of the physical pain and anguish of being treated as a "thing" - the treatment was sanctioned by her mother.

My stepfather attempted, on many occasions, to molest me. I managed to elude him since I was smarter than he was and I have a 6th sense about danger.

I told my mother what was happening assuming she'd step in and save me.

Instead, she advised me, "Don't try to come between me and my husband."

I knew then that I was on my own. I was 9 years old. At that instant I felt the world drop out under my feet; I was left hanging in space.

Every night I would push my big, heavy dresser over my door to block the entrance and I'd sit, talking to my dog, so anyone would know I was awake.

I was a nervous wreck; I became extremely defensive and hostile. At one church I attended when I was12, the pastor's wife had me over for tea. I was very suspicious why anyone would have *me* over for tea, why would anyone be nice to *me* - what was she up to?

I had no self-respect. I understood I wasn't wanted as a girl; I was a "thing" that my mother had to keep, put up with, as a necessary evil, but I was not loved or wanted. My mother assumed she'd have a son and when I arrived she was deeply disappointed - wouldn't even name me - my cousins did.

So, an invitation to tea from the pastor's wife had me wary, alerted… why would anyone be nice to me - I had no value…what was she up to?

I went to her home, sat in the edge of a chair - "on edge." She chatted- I sat, waiting for bad news, frozen with fear. What was she up to? My defense antennae were on high searching for a clue to "what had I done now to be punished for…?"

The pastor's wife spoke gently, kindly and managed to weave a question into the conversation, "How are things at home?"

My antennae snapped to attention - in no way would I betray my nightmare life at "home". I would never tell how I pushed my dresser against my bedroom door to keep it shut, how I sat up all night, on guard, hugging my dog, talking to my dog so my stepfather would know I was awake. How I took baths at night with the bathroom lights out and only went to the bathroom if he weren't home. He had drilled holes in the bathroom and my bedroom walls and ceilings to spy on me.

If someone at school talked to me or touched me I jumped a foot and responded with a hostile comment. My tongue was sharp - I could easily push people away with caustic barbs - my defense weapons.

I responded to her covert question, "How are things at home…?" by a curt, "Fine!" and said no more, walked home, shivering in fear. What was she up to?

Now, I know. She was trying to be nice. Many times since then I have shed tears at the thought someone was being nice to me - she was sincere. Maybe she actually cared…

Much later, I was a divorced mother with 2 daughters. One daughter had been in a serious accident and was brain-damaged. I came home early from work one day to find my stepfather having sex with my brain-damaged daughter.

I was hysterical and attempted to kill him. My mother got between us to protect him. I went, in my hysteria, to the priest at church and sobbed out the story. His advice?

"Get over it."

Men bond. A priest is a man first, priest second.

I moved out. My mother committed suicide.

My stepfather got remarried and moved on.

Of what use is #MeToo when women, our mothers, pave the way for men to injure us, insult us, use us, degrade us? How can we move forward when we allow ourselves, our daughters, to be so cheapened and abused? Our daughters, other women, represent us; we are one concept. But, we are lumped together as "second class," "helpmeets." When we down-grade our self, we downgrade all humanity. As we get dragged down in society, so everyone, by default, goes with us.

Does God play favorites?

The Priest represents God. If God says "get over it" it must be of no consequence - it's a girl, who cares! And, by what means can a celibate priest understand the interaction between married people and families - understand the conflict of gender?

How can he understand a helpless, terrified little girl?

Until you have personally experienced the joys, sorrows, upheavals in a marriage, how can you understand the anguish or joy of that interaction? Each marriage is unique, convoluted, and each person brings the past with him or her which complicates the perceptions and interaction many times over.

As an aside, at this time there is considerable news exposure of thousands of children who have been molested by priests. There is a hue and cry for priests to be married. But, if 7 out of 10 fathers molest their daughters and many of the priests are gay and molest boys, what is the advantage in priests being married? It would not affect the behavior of deviants in any way.

Too often when a man insults a woman, demeans her, touches her inappropriately, some other woman will stand up for him, "Well, you must have misunderstood." "That wasn't right." "Are you sure?" "Well, he's always been good to me!"

The woman is shut down.

No outrage. No condemning his bad behavior; no "hearing" what the girl is saying. Often the woman listening will change the subject, "Well, he shouldn't have done that. I know we need change… how's the meatloaf…?"

Is the #Me Too movement just another gentle tap on the male hand, a frown, a tip of our head to indicate displeasure?

In the women's writing class, one woman wrote about her home life with her grandfather. She told her mother that her grandfather was molesting her and her sister (11 and 9 years old). With a sigh of resignation the mother replied, "Yes. He had sex with me and my sisters, too, while we were growing up."

End of problem. End of discussion.

The mother had a "position," a socially acceptable standing in the community - she was not about to give that up just for her daughter's safety! The "Mrs." - the mothers of incest victims, have an unspoken agreement - they hide together behind a mask.

Their solidarity assumes the mask of resignation, save the illusion of a happy marriage at all costs, save the illusion of security, the illusion that the mother is doing a good job.

"Happily" married women allow, sanction, their daughters being molested. They know what's going on! When interviewed about her daughter's trauma with being molested by her father, the mother said, "I thought he'd stop." Really?

The problem is hidden behind a facade of happiness - they're good women married to good men - Christians! They sacrifice their daughter to save face for the man - as well as the mothers' security - her identity - her position in the community.

When I'd complain about my stepfather to my mother, she'd say, "He's a good man." I had no rebuttal - why bother?

My personal feelings about "Christian" men who molest their daughters, is that God has a special place in Hell for them. They know better! They have NO excuse to harm anyone! Especially a girl, their daughter, is a special charge, by God, for them to take care of! This situation is particularly heinous!

To protect girls from their father sends the message men are not trustworthy, imperfect; then, what does that say about the woman who married him? Does the message say she's a loser, stupid, incompetent? What's wrong with her? Can a woman stand up under that scrutiny?

Also, if women sanction, disbelieve - or, overlook - fathers molesting their daughters, the concept of fear and disgust can be easily transferred to the definition of God. We're told to "fear" God. "love" God, "respect" God - our "father." It's a sin not to "love" the Father. How can the child "love" someone who terrorizes her? Can you imagine the child's confusion?

I read an abstract of an incest occurrence. The young daughter of a psychologist was molested by her father, the husband of the psychologist. They separated. The mother went to another psychologist for advice as to what to do about visiting rights. She was told to allow the father to see the child on a regular basis as it would be "advantageous" for the child.

The mother then searched for data and professional guidance from other studies in child molesting. There was no data; there were some case descriptions, only.

I have a degree in Psychology; it's a necessary discipline - we need to understand motives, goals and backgrounds of disturbed people to guide them to a more productive way of living - this should include ourselves.

But…

The study of behavior is wide open to conjecture, supposition. We observe aberrant behavior and muse, "Maybe it's…," "I think…," "Let's try…," "Hmmmm…." You cannot always anticipate or control what behavior will surface under what conditions. The experiments in mind-perception are not repeatable, nor reliable, in many cases when we treat someone. Much of therapy is projection - opinion, by the therapist. Therapists should have a label stuck on their forehead, "Warning, use cautiously, take everything I say with a big dose of skepticism."

But…

As a desperate measure we can always fall back on Common Sense. Unfortunately, there are no degrees, studies or research in Common Sense. I doubt there's two similar definitions.

If the father is allowed to see the daughter it should be under adult supervision; they should *never be left alone.* And, as a completely outrageous thought, we might ask the daughter her opinion, how does she feel about seeing her father again…? Did anyone think to ask the girl - or boy, the child, how he/she feels?

Or, by tradition, would we immediately negate or ignore her response…excuse, justify the father's position?

There's the old advice about falling of a horse; if you fall off a horse, get right back on and keep going - get over the fear right away. But, the fear from being molested is not like "falling off a horse," your soul is wounded - bruises heal, but a soul never heals.

MALE RIVALRY: COMPETITION AT ITS LOWEST FORM

In general, men are competitive. At times competition is healthy, normal, exciting, stimulating and can have a lasting, positive effect on society.

Other times, it's incredibly stupid.

There have been cases where, when a man's wife was pregnant, he assumed all the symptoms of pregnancy, early morning vomiting, back pains, irritability - whatever his wife can do, he can do better.

Of course the symptoms are real, the pregnancy is not. But when a man wants attention, reality - common sense, flies out the window.

He wants attention, *all of it*, and, NOW!

Oh, yes, his wife might be pregnant - but not like he is! He's *really* sick!

Even with postpartum blues he suffers excruciating symptoms - far stronger than his wife.

And I found out, it's the same with menopause.

My friend, Joe, in his treatment of cancer, was getting estrogen shots. Joe was in his late 60's and the shots were causing the "change of life" - menopause - he said.

He complained about hot-flashes; how he suffered, hot-cold…cold-hot. He described them minutely for my understanding. Annoyed, I said, "Yes. Woman have been having these for thousands of years!"

"Ah, but," he replied. "No woman has ever had hot flashes like these."

I guess that's possible…

FAIRY TALES - their covert message

Fairy tales are covert messages passed down through millennia to encourage women to "wake up" and assume their rightful place in society. Their "rightful" place of being 1/2 of any society, 1/2 of any population, is a position of power or dominance. The prince kisses the beauty to wake her up.

The kiss is a symbol of males agreeing to, *a partner,* in the "awakening" of female power; a recognition of the rights of women *beside men* in Life. The kiss is a "coming together in peace," a "standing beside your partner." When you remain submissive, you are not "awake," you're a zombie.

Other interpretations of the "kiss" are that it is the sexual awakening of women. Good grief - sex again? How did they figure that out? Sex is submissive on the part of the woman -

usually- What good does it do to "awaken" if you're still submissive? I understand some women sleep through sex…

If one bases the kiss on Carl Jung's analysis instead of Freud, the interpretation might read that the kiss is a transference of power; it's permission to come "awake" and take your place in Life, be a power that stands beside power. In the Collective Unconscious is it possible that all humans have a desire, a need, to share in power - to be recognized, respected, appreciated? Aren't *all ideas,* creativity, energy, accessible in the Collective Unconscious?

Is the Collective Unconscious gender-related? Selective? Or in the vast Universe are not all ideas, all minds, connected?

Isn't getting pregnant yearly, having thriving brothels from the beginning of time and society's insistence on "heirs," - a woman's "duty," a sign that women are already "sexually awakened"? Don't we already know what our bits and pieces are for?

In the story of Blue Beard, in his castle he had the only key to the door of a secret room. His (current) wife stole the key (freedom) and opened forbidden door (the "kiss," the "awakening"). Inside the secret room were dozens of mummified bodies of previous wives. She knew she'd be next. Her brothers arrived at a critical moment, slew Blue Beard and saved her.

Her brothers freed her, like the prince's kiss in other fairy tales. In slaying her captive, she is released - awakened - into freedom for herself.

In the story "1001 Nights," Sheherazade marries the Sultan who kills all his wives in the morning after the wedding night. It's his way of getting even with one of his wives who left him for another man.

Sheherzade manages to win over the Sultan by her wit; the stories are the "kiss," the awakening of her power over the Sultan. She frees herself.

The point of the "fairy tales" is that the woman is free, but she PARTNERS with the other half! She is as equal in stature and value as the male half.

We do not need to be "awakened" to sex! We need to be awakened to the strength of our own power and place in this world.

I am always disappointed when sex is insinuated into an analysis - well, it actually might be a factor - but *always*…? Freud started it all. He said women have penis envy, want to be males. I used to wonder about his conclusion that this was our problem - we want a penis.

A woman wants her husband to respect her and stop beating her. Freud says she want a penis…what we *really* want is a penis…?

When a housewife goes shopping what she *really* wants is a product that is accessible, long-lasting performance and is satisfying.

Apparently Freud didn't do the shopping.

Our input in decision-making, policy-making in major issues is essential and valuable. When creating a direction for any population, there should be representatives from all levels of society. Decision-making should not be lop-sided toward male opinion, male needs and male convenience.

The census of most countries shows women to be a dominant force in numbers. Therefore, our voice should be - if not "dominant" - strongly attended to.

The covert message is:

Sleeping Beauty, wake up! Snow white, wake up!

Cinderella, put down your broom! Rapunzel - get a trim!

WOMEN! WAKE UP!

Take your rightful place as intelligent decision-makers of your gender's rights - take control of your Life!

Don't *ask* for your rights…**TAKE THEM!**

Men *have* rights - women want to share them.

There's **NO SHARING!** We want the whole steak! Claim your rights and move forward.

ABORTION

Perhaps the most divisive issue ever to come before Americans is the question of abortion - to be, or, not to be?

This one issue separates us into camps of "freedom of choice," or, "sin." There is a strong element of society that believes pregnancy is "punishment" for Eve "forcing" Adam to "eat of the fruit."

So, if Eve (the "sinner") can control her reproduction and chooses not to bear a baby due to rape, lust, innocence or accident, many people consider her freedom to choose an unforgivable sin - she must be punished!

Those people considering abortion to be a "sin," they state the vast numbers of people wanting to adopt. According to them, there are lines of desperate people surrounding adoption agencies anxiously hoping to adopt a baby.

That is a total lie.

People want perfect babies, beautiful babies, and, they have to be *babies,* not the older children who may have psychological problems. There are so many conflicting reports about adoption. It is perhaps a good idea to get a qualified attorney who understands the adoption process and will help you find the right child, should you choose to adopt.

Let's agree, abortion, unless under critical situations, is **WRONG.** If at all possible you may want to get a qualified attorney help you find trustworthy options.

Birth control is ***RIGHT.*** There's no qualification here; birth control is *right.*

But, the moralists and fundamentalists are against even that. How cold-blooded and hateful can people be? Pregnancy should not be a "punishment" - it should be a welcomed, joyful event!

This is one of the areas of #MeToo, Women's Lib and Just Say No movements we must attend to. We must head in the direction of *education,* not continue to wander in darkness, a hit-or-miss philosophy.

RAPE - A TWO-WAY STREET "What did you do to bring this on?"

I sometimes wonder just how far from the tree we have really fallen - are we actually "civilized" or just prehensile beings in haute couture?

Do prehensile beings "rape," or is that just a homo Erectus hobby? It is definitely not homo Sapiens behavior - that is - if we're "sapiens" at all.

By this time in "civilization," we women know that if we wear dresses that reveal our personal body parts we will probably excite and attract the attention of the male gender. On occasion this excitement gets out of control.

We know this. And yet we continue to wear pieces of leisure wear, or formal wear, that leave major chunks of our anatomy on display. From past experiences, we know that these body parts will excite the id in males and result in violent, unwelcome reproductive acts.

We taunt, he responds - we complain.

We get what we ask for.

And, no, all women do not do this, we try to be reasonably modest and well-groomed. Yes, most of us do.

Our assumption, as women is, "I have on the latest style; this is the color that brings out my eyes - he will focus on my eyes - the ad said so."

> *Bikini swimsuits had just come in vogue and my twin girls wanted one - everyone was getting them. We stood at the swimsuit rack at Penney's surrounded by mothers with young girls. My girls were asking, "Please, please, can we get bikini's?" That was not going to happen! I said, "No! You're not for sale!" The other mothers were horrified at what I said! Too bad!*

In general girls are fun, nice, bright and energetic. Some of them are thin, wear clothes well and look good in anything. Some of them don't. Girls should wear their skirts long enough to cover their legs to just above the knees - no shorter.

Blouses should cover everything except the neck and the holes for the arms. This of course is not reality. But, as it stands, the tops are fa-a-r too low and the skirts fa-a-r too short. I can hardly bring myself to mention the short shorts - they are MOST unflattering!

When girls walk, bend over, go upstairs, their gender is displayed to anyone within a block around them. This means men; men who look at girls and think, "They want it - they know they want it;" they're "asking for it."

And, from the perspective of men, they're right.

On the news an older librarian complained one of the members of the library, a young man, had a camera and was taking photos of her anatomy up under her dress.

I thought, "Today you can take photos up a dress from across the street." If it's so easy to film your personal accessories, maybe your dress is the wrong length for you.

If you wear provocative clothes, don't complain when you get unwanted advances.

I was at a wedding of a couple in their 20's. The bride had never worn a dress before; it was a new experience. She walked down the aisle trying hard to manage the dress, flowers and shoes.

The top of the bridesmaid "dresses" was just above the lowest part of their breasts. None of the girls was slender - it was obvious they were well-fed.

The hemline was just above the very top of their legs. It was most unattractive. It looked like the girls were wearing a wide sash and forgot to put on the skirt.

This image is what the guests took home with them.

Where are the mothers? The fathers? Someone with a functioning brain cell?

The family gathered at Uncle Leo's for a BBQ. His 30 year old married daughter was saying, "Dad, when I was a teen ager and I'd come to you and ask if I could go somewhere, if you didn't think it was right, you'd say, 'No,' and I couldn't go. I just wanted to thank you for that because often I didn't want to go, but this way I could use you as an excuse. Thank you." What a great Dad!

FIVE REASONS WE FAIL TO HAVE RESPECT

I promised you 5 reasons why any movement towards respect, freedom, encouragement will not work, and here they are:

1. Women allow their daughters to be molested by their husbands and boy friends and lie about it, don't report it or stop it.

2. Women do not support other women.

3. Women are still the butt of jokes (blondes, mothers-in-law).

4. Sexual harassment is covered up, on-the-job, at school, home. Poo poo'ed (You "misunderstood." "What did you do to encourage it?")

5. Women prefer their sons; leave them the estate in toto.

6. Women want everyone to have a chance, forgive the transgressors.

7. Women will sell their soul to get a husband, go into bondage. We compete for the privilege of being shack-led.

8. Women do not take women seriously; we're ignored for advice in the corporate world - and at home.

9. Women blame women for bringing it on themselves - "You should have known…" "You should have…" "Well, if you had just…"

10. We forgive.

("He didn't mean it…" "He just needs a chance…" "Maybe you misunderstood…")

No. If someone has transgressed, you pin *that person* down and address the situation in basic, elementary terms: "See Dick run, see Spot run…" - you don't excuse it, understand it or "give another chance."

You STOP IT! - THERE AND THEN!

11. "God" will be displeased.

Who told you that? Did God, *personally*, say vis a vis, "You have to allow yourself to be insulted, denigrated, humiliated, ridiculed… because Eve bit that apple?!" Or, have we been told, to "love (respect) your neighbor **as yourself**!"

Humans are a work of Love, a work of art to be respected. If we are insulted we must correct the problem. But, we also must not insult others - that's fair.

We must take charge of our lives, NOW, or, stay at square one. Our need for respect is long overdue. It's *our* choice. It's *our* problem.

We should start, from Day 1, with babies, how to be respectful to self and others.

TESTOSTERONE VS ESTROGEN

Science has satisfactorily determined that estrogen is a hormone which has a calming effect on an individual. People using estrogen for physical or mental disturbances are usually calmer and happier after treatment.

Testosterone, on the other hand is for people who need energy and it helps in mental acuity, making decisions and encourages inner strength - the belief in ones' self.

In one abstract I read, a housewife, who was incapable of making decisions, couldn't reason out problems, couldn't find the car keys, her eyeglasses, who let people walk over her and take advantage of her, decided to allow researchers to experiment with her into taking injections of testosterone.

The researchers wanted to see if that hormone would have any effect on her mental acuity and self perception.

It did.

After injections, the housewife turned into a totally different person. She walked holding herself up straight; she looked people in the eyes when she spoke and talked in a louder, firm voice. She made decisions - unhesitating decisions, "Yes!," and "NO!" and felt alive for the first time in her life.

She was so happy with her new-found inner strength that she refused to give up the injections.

Then, some time ago I read an abstract about a study of male prisoners in Pelican Bay, a high security prison in California.

The population of this prison is reputed to be one of the most dangerous and feared prisons in America. The remedy for violent behavior in a man was a stay in isolation which reduced him to the lowest level of human behavior.

A group of scientists decided to experiment on some of these men to see if it were possible to lessen, remove or modify their violent behavior by injecting a series of estrogen shots.

A group of 6 men volunteered to accept the estrogen shots; they agreed to be used in the experiment. After awhile the hormone shots took effect. These violent, reactive men, fearless fighters, remorseless killers who defended their manhood and reputation to the death, became calm, happy and relaxed. They were no longer defensive or have a chip on their shoulder.

But…the problem was, they grew breasts.

Very few men will allow themselves to sport breasts. The experiments were halted. But the point was proven; behavior can be drastically altered by hormone therapy.

Estrogen calms you down; testosterone peps you up. Which could extrapolate the conclusion that women will never be "fighters," and men will never be happy doing their nails.

We will always be who we are - women defending bad behavior and men strongly competitive.

As an aside, can you imagine two felons having a chat after their estrogen shots:

"Excuse me, Strangler. Which hors d'oeuvre do you recommend with the aperitif?"

"Oh, Mad Dog, I suggest the anchovy paste canapé - it has a soupçon of garlic."

And the woman with the testosterone shots opens a bottle of beer with her teeth.

WHAT ARE WE (still) TEACHING GIRLS TODAY?

"If you can't say anything nice, don't say anything at all."

"Just be nice to them and they'll be nice to you."

Yes, Dorothy, let's hold hands and go skipping down the yellow brick road.

I took a self-defense class at the "Y." About 12 of us women were lined up in front of a heavily padded man who we were supposed to kick somehow - I forget the details. A woman had her late teen-aged daughter in line to kick, but she couldn't. She didn't want to hurt him. She just stood in front of him, frozen, while the rest of us (im) patiently waited our turn. We never got a turn - I was so annoyed. This was a self-defense class! We learned nothing! Isn't the job of the Instructor to force us to act? If we wait for the girl to defend herself she goes down and so do we - the attacker ain't gonna wait!

The girl was taught to be nice. That's hard to erase. Maybe she should try testosterone.

RESPECT: AS TAUGHT BY DONALD TRUMP, PRESIDENT OF THE UNITED STATES OF AMERICA

In this quote Mr. Trump explained his method of interacting at his level of prestige with the wife of another prestigious public minister:

> "I moved on her like a bitch. But I couldn't get there. and she was married you know? I am attracted to beautiful - I just start kissing them it's like a magnet. Just kiss. I don't even wait. And when you're a star they let you do it. You can do anything, grab 'em by the pussy you can do anything.

Oct. 7, 2016 "Access Hollywood"

When this quote was on the news, women were outraged at Donald Trump for his attitude toward women. I was more outraged at the woman for allowing herself to be insulted. But, she was not insulted - she was a participant. It was the other millions of women in America who were insulted. Because she "easily" allowed the President to demean her, it can be extrapolated that all women are "easy."

My guess is she was "whoring" for her husband; they can keep their political position and status as long as she "cooperates."

THE OTHER SIDE OF THE COIN

Women demand respect; men assume it. Women want someone to "give" them respect. No one "gives" you respect. You live and breathe respect in your own life, create it, think it, be it, use it. You expect respect and settle for nothing less than the best!

Don't wait and hope someone will "*give* you respect." Live respectfully!

We cannot be respected when we dress to deliberately attract men. We appear obvious, desperate and easy. We put ourselves on a action block to be viewed as "available, price reduced." We make fools of ourselves following "fashion." We wear dresses so our gender is obvious and apparent.

When our bait is so obvious, it's a turn-off to the hunter. Men don't like to be stalked; they see themselves as hunters who bag the game by clever maneuvering and strength of their manhood. If those attributes are not honored, the men move camp to a place where the hunt is more of a challenge.

They dump the easy girl and look for a "trophy." We send the message that we're glad to please men for any price and under any conditions. Often if the bait, the prize, is a challenge to trap, that prize becomes more valuable; the challenge is a test of his testosterone level - his personal value.

In one of my classes a young female student had an enormous bosom. She was a very nice girl, who, I doubt understood the impact of her charms. At one time, in front of the class, she wore a simple blouse that was cut modestly low in front, but when giving a speech, she leaned over to reach a visual aid. As she bent over to pick up the item, her breasts oozed out of her low-cut blouse and they never stopped oozing.

The class went dead silent. I about died from embarrassment. In fact, I thought the room might tip over at that side from the imbalance of weight - I hung on to my desk. It took a few moments for the class to recover - if they ever did.

This particular student was a sweet girl. I wish someone had the courage to suggest she wear her blouses somewhat higher - by about 3 inches, at least. As her instructor, I was hesitant to say anything and overstep my professional boundary.

This is all I remember of her. How many times is this scenario repeated, where, all one remembers about someone is the inappropriate outfit they were wearing? So sad and so easily fixed.

Don't these people have mothers?

Years ago when I shopped at high-end dress shops a woman fashion consultant was available to suggest what to wear and what not to wear. She was diplomatic but firm in her suggestions. It would be a great service to women if a store would employ these advisers again today.

About now someone will comment, "Women have the right to dress as they want to." And I would totally agree, but…

Here's where the problem comes in.

Mark Judge (close friend of Brett Kavanaugh) said the way women dress leads to rape. There's no denying that; the clothes a woman does or, does not wear, tells us who she is.

Some men perceive women dressed for "action," and then they think we all want "action." Apparently the male brain is incapable of discrimination. Many men observe a women and assume, "You know you want it - you know you do." These men assume if there are women who dress to display themselves, then all women dress to display themselves - the men don't distinguish one woman from another - we all "want it." All women want a man, any man, any way they can get one; we all look alike.

Because some women dress to advertise sex, there are men who assume this is how all women dress even if we're wearing astronaut gear - we're all the same. As my husband used to say, "Turn women upside down and they're all sisters." That was just before he left me for a "sister;" I found out later I had a lot of "sisters." I'll bet my "sister" has a "sister" at this moment.

When I was a girl, women had their body parts covered to some degree, and we managed just fine to attract men (you will notice the exponential increase of population over the years); women who dressed in good taste were held in esteem by both men and women.

"Esteem" is another word for "respect."

NO ESCAPING ANNOYING BOYS

As a young girl in school, I usually understood all lessons literally. If you made a comment to me, I took it literally, "Carolyn, take a chair." I'd take a chair, hold it and wonder what to do with it. The nuns were always upset with me - they thought I was being funny. No, I wasn't - I was confused.

In music class was a song about how boys annoyed girls. I found boys very annoying; they chased me around at recess, pulled my braids and one even knocked me down for no reason.

So when this song suggested we could get rid of them by going overseas I had hope I'd be left in peace. Then I was disappointed because all the boys "would follow after like a swarm of bumblebees." I just wanted to be left alone.

"Rubin, Rubin, I've Been Thinking"

Traditional Song

Reuben, Reuben, I've been thinking. What a strange world this would be If the men were all transported Far beyond the northern sea!

Rachel, Rachel, I've been thinking. What a strange world this would be If the girls were all transported Far beyond the northern sea!

Reuben, Reuben, I've been thinking. Life would be so easy then! What a great world this would be, If there were no tiresome men!

Rachel, Rachel, I've been thinking. Life would be so easy then! What a great world this would be, If you'd leave it to the men!

Reuben, Reuben, I've been thinking. If we went beyond the seas, All the men would follow after Like a swarm of bumblebees!

Rachel, Rachel, I've been thinking. If we went beyond the seas, All the girls all would follow after Like a swarm of honeybees!

As a child, the lyrics of this song gave me a sense of futility; if I ever tried to escape, some man would swim after me to annoy me. I wonder if the boys felt the same way - stalked…

WOMEN SWIM AFTER MEN

When a woman wants a man the common phrases are: Catch a man, hook a man, grab a man, get a man, bait him, find a man - the implication being that a man is an animal that must be trapped, deluded and tricked into marriage.

This is grossly insulting for him and for us. If we want respect, it has to go both ways. Men are the prize, the goal, of many, many women. Those women are consumed with finding "a" man. But, think about it - if we feel a man is equal to a dumb animal to be trapped and skinned, what does that say about us?

Have we so little self-pride we have to put ourselves on an animal level along with our "mate" (I hate that word - apes have "mates" - not people!)?

There were two women and a man, all in their 50's. "Noreen" was married to "Axel" and "Doris" wanted him. Axel couldn't make up his mind which woman he wanted. So for over a year Axel would alternate sleeping at one woman's house, have breakfast there; then have dinner and sleep at the other house that night. The women took turns entertaining Axel, but Doris, the one I knew, was pretty sure she'd "win" him. She did. Triumphant, she told me goodbye; they left, forever, on his motorcycle.

Another woman, "Delilah," wanted "a" man. She was in her early 60's, divorced, but financially secure. She joined several date clubs, searched on line, went weekly to various psychics who all told her he was "near by at a lake." All she had to do was pluck a pink rose at the full moon, dip it in water from the Ganges while hopping on one foot. She spent over $3,000 a month looking for psychic guidance as well as going to dating sites and clubs.

WHITE MALES AND THEIR SUICIDE RATE

Current research in America shows a spike in white male suicide of men in their fifties and older. Their suicide rate shows that 7 out of 10 older white men have found life intolerable and have taken their own lives.

This data is extraordinary - it's considered an "epidemic." At this time, there are no specific reasons known as to why this is happening. The men leave no note nor any indication of how they feel or have any message for their family or friends.

To me, this lack of communication indicates complete despair, a feeling of isolation, emptiness. To not explain "why" to your family is complete abandonment of them and your identity, your link to Life.

This behavior is drastic, completely out of character for older white males. What would make them want to leave life anonymously? Quietly? Alone?

Did they feel abandoned? Helpless? Useless…? Unloved… we'll never know. But, social researchers need reasons why a phenomenon happens so we can cure it or counter it.

So, researchers have tentatively focused on the women's liberation movement as a possible cause. The suicides are a current phenomenon and women's lib is a current phenomenon also. Perhaps they're linked?

The theory is that, because of women achieving personal and social power, men have lost face; the power they've lost is the power women gained - took, stole.

This theory assumes that Face, Power and Status are finite; there's only 2 pounds to go 'round for each person. If we (women's lib) take 1 1/2 lbs of FPS, then white men, 50 yrs and older, don't get their full share - they get cheated out of what's theirs, 1 lb. of FPS.

Men don't notice - or care - that the women's share of FPS has been always been 3 ounces or less. But "fair" is not the issue here; the issue is **respect.** Face, Power and Status are fine, if that's a woman's goal. But recognition - respect is our basic issue, for everyone.

For eons white males have been in control, ruled, decided the fate of thousands of souls, arbitrarily - for the men's convenience. Now they have to share, and they don't know how. White males (too often) have shown a lack of concern for others; they're used to being petted, obeyed, enjoyed self focus and respect.

Proof of their value is their impressive income, perks, status and support system - all self-administered.

In a way, their despair, loss of life's purpose, is tentatively our fault - the fault of women's lib. If we had any respect for ourselves, we would never have allowed this imbalance of power exist for so long.

There will be those women, people, among us who feel that if we went back to being submissive and cow'ed, men would not feel the need for suicide.

In China, according to statistics, one million women per year, *1,000,000 per year,* attempt suicide. Ten thousand succeed - *TEN THOUSAND* - Per year.

Does anyone care?

Is there any data on how many American women, black and white, commit suicide, or attempt it? Are there any studies as to why American women want to die?

Is women's suicide a phenomenon - or just business as usual?

Does anyone care?

THE HAND THAT ROCKS THE CRA-DLE RULES THE WORLD

Recently on the news, a boy of about 15 yrs old murdered his girl friend, strangled her. One of his friends, another boy of about 15 yrs old, was being interviewed on the news.

When asked why his friend would murder a young girl, the second young man shrugged his shoulders and said, "Boys will be boys."

Exactly what does that mean?

Bad behavior is inherent, intractable? It's ordained? It's sanctioned?

Is there a cure? A prevention?

Who's in control of raising the young men? Who's teaching them to respect others, restrain the id, control the "self"?

Instead of teaching respect for others, control of self, restraint in anger - are we teaching, "If it feels good to you - just do it."?

But then, when someone does a "just do it" to you, you put up a howl because it's not fair?

It's a difficult job to teach children to respect others and respect yourself also. Where and when do you draw the line for aggression? Under what circumstances does a child recognize as dangerous or innocent?

I was standing at the top of an escalator with my handicapped daughter ready to start down. My daughter is very unsteady but can manage her balance if there's no obstacle in her way. A baby about 10 months old was sitting at the base of the escalator watching the steps come down and fold into the floor. The grandparents, I assume the older couple, were standing about 6 feet away watching the baby on the floor. The escalator was moving down, relentlessly and, concerned for my daughter's safety, I yelled at the older couple, "HEY! Get that baby out of the way! My daughter is handicapped!" They didn't move but continued like "American Gothic" to stand, frozen and stare at the baby. I yelled again - angry, "Get that baby out of there! My daughter is handicapped!" Nothing. I ran down the stairs, grabbed the baby by the collar and pulled it back just in time for my daughter to wobble off the escalator. The older couple never reacted. Is this "training" for the future of us all?

My husband, as the chef in our home, kept his knives extraordinarily sharp. We had visitors, husband and wife and their son, 12 years old. In the kitchen, the son picked up a knife and started wielding it like a saber, slash! Slash! in our narrow kitchen with four adults standing talking. I yelled, "Put the knife down! It's very sharp!" He continued to "slash!" Again, I yelled, "Put the knife down - it's SHARP!" The parents stood there, staring straight ahead, blank faces. I grabbed the kid's wrist, slammed it down on the counter and took away the knife. No reaction from either parent!

Who's in charge these days? Who's the parent? And we're surprised when children shoot children…

FIRST-BORN GIRLS vs boys

A friend told me about a recent study of families who had children of boys and girls. In the families that had girls born first, older than the sons, the boys were taught restraint, patience, sensitivity and sharing by the older girls.

Everyone got along quite well. When a disturbance started, the mother quietly stepped in and stopped the fuss. It was a master stroke of controlled control.

FIRST-BORN BOYS vs girls

I think the results of this study are not necessarily genetic, I believe they are the result of the *lack* of learning, the *lack* of teaching. Some children are more energetic than others, thus they seem more "aggressive."

In families where the boys were first born, the girls suffered a great deal for the torment and ridicule the parents *allowed* the boys to do. So many people think boys should be rowdy, should be out-of-control, its supposedly their nature.

Maybe it is. But shouldn't we, the "adults," handle any aggression in a mature manner? Demonstrate patience, understanding. Boy, it ain't easy!

My friend, Hazel, and I taught anti-bullying classes at the YMCA. We had one little boy brought in by a concerned father. No one would play with this child - he had no friends. He was over-the-top energetic trying too hard to be friends. It wasn't "aggression," it was misdirected aggression.

We showed him how to say "Hi!" without hitting someone to get their attention. We demonstrated easier, shorter arm and hand movements so that he didn't "scare" the other kids. He got the idea and both he and the father went home with some better idea of how to control energy.

When we allow children to express aggression, grabbing, pushing, hitting and laughing at others, we are teaching young men how to run-over the rights of others, how to grope, handle, insult others - girls in particular.

By the time they're teens and aggression has jelled, we think, that's the way they are, can't fix it. Girls just have to deal with being raped, laughed at… Really?

If we can train elephants to dance we can train males to be courteous.

Until women cooperate with each other, support each other, see themselves as worthy, intelligent and valuable people, all of society will continue wallow in separation, fear, imbalance of power and the degradation of 1/2 of the population.

Women will stay at Square One. Is this why God put us here?

"The past is prologue to the future."

Shakespeare

ABOUT THE AUTHOR

Carolyn Franklin

M.A. Communication Studies

M. A. Education

B. A. Psychology

Opera singer, Bel Canto method

Private coach voice/speech development

Conduct Communication seminars

Conduct classes in Carl Orff Reading Readiness

Life Choices Consultant

voicedynamicscf@yahoo.com

OTHER BOOKS BY CAROLYN FRANKLIN

Adam: First Man or First Mouse?

Athena: Goddess of Communication Strategies

Attorneys: Public Speaking

Coping With Bullies: A gentle approach

E-Z Dictionary: Use the Right, Rite, Wright, Write Word

Emotional Intelligence

Just Be Yourself, Whoever That Is!

Public Speaking Made Easier

RX For Your Communication Ills

The Story of Mary: Mayhem, Mirth and Miracles

You Can Catch More Flies With Honey

Your Voice Your Personality

Women At Work: Win-Win Strategies

Women Bullying Women